Vampires

of Lore

A. P. SYLVIA

Vampires

# of Lore

TRAITS

AND MODERN

MISCONCEPTIONS

SCHIFFER
PUBLISHING

4880 Lower Valley Road · Atglen, PA 19310

Contents

Preface

With its bright lights, flashing billboards, and throngs of people, Times Square in New York City may seem like an unusual place to bring up at the start of a vampire book. However, it was there that, quite by accident, I began my journey into the legends and folklore surrounding the undead. Among the various sights and sounds of this world-famous square is an attraction that offers all kinds of curiosities to behold: a Ripley's Believe It or Not! museum.

I found myself standing in front of it one night during a visit to New York City, and I just knew I had to go inside. Among all the strange objects I saw, one exhibit really struck me. Sitting behind a glass display case sat a wooden box that held a variety of unusual tools, such as a wooden stake, a cross, and vials of various substances. It also held a pistol, complete with silver bullet and bullet mold. Produced by a Professor Blomberg, the object was described as a nineteenth-century vampire killing kit. Apparently, these kits were sold to travelers heading to eastern Europe. Its aged appearance, strange contents, and fantastic backstory made it instantly memorable for me.

After returning home from that visit, my mind started drifting back to this strange artifact, and I found myself wanting to learn more about it. So, like anyone who wants to get questions answered these days, I took to the internet. It didn't take much searching for me to realize that there was some controversy surrounding these objects. While Ripley's maintains that the kits are genuine—and it actually owns a number of them[1]—there are some people who dispute the authenticity of such items. For example, Jonathan Ferguson, curator of firearms at the Royal Armouries in the UK, has stated that there is no evidence for the use of vampire killing kits. In regard to the Blomberg ones, he feels that their components, though antique, seem to reflect fiction and film. He is of the opinion that these kits probably weren't assembled before the 1930s, and it's likely they came into existence when vampire movies from Hammer Films were popular.[2] (For reference, Hammer released its first vampire-themed movie in 1958.)

This notion of the kit's contents reflecting film rather than folklore brought me to a bigger question. I started wondering how our modern vampire characters compared to the actual beliefs and superstitions of the past. How much do we really know about the true folkloric vampire, the kind that haunted the nightmares of people generations ago? Anyone who has watched a documentary about these things probably has some sense that the bloodsucker of today has evolved over time. This notion was certainly familiar to me, since I've long been interested in supernatural beliefs. However, I wanted to dig deep on this topic (six feet at least). I thought it would be fascinating to analyze today's vampires, trait by trait, and determine if there were folkloric precedents for them. If I couldn't find any, then I wanted to know when and how the trait was originally introduced. Ultimately, what began as some simple web searching turned into the book before you.

The task of deconstructing the vampire actually proved more challenging than expected. One thing I realized early on was that I had to be very careful in terms of my sources. On occasion, I noticed that some discussions about vampire folklore contained details that were commonly associated with fictional vampires. When I then looked up the same stories in older sources, those details were missing. It seemed that later researchers, knowingly or not, injected some modern tropes into their work. To avoid being misled by what I jokingly called the "Dracula Effect," I decided to use pre-twentieth-century sources whenever possible. My hope was that there was less chance of these books being contaminated by contemporary expectations. When using modern sources, I tried to lean on works that were scholarly in nature, if available.

One other challenge I encountered was when a writer would assert something about vampires, but it wasn't clear where exactly their information was coming from. In this book, I've made an effort to provide precise citations for all the vampire accounts and traditions I discuss. For those readers who are curious to learn more, I hope you'll find it easy to do so by using my sources.

I'm quite happy that I wandered into Ripley's that day. It ended up sending me down a fascinating path. Besides all my reading and research, I also found opportunities to connect with this history in more-tangible ways. For example, I visited a number of cemeteries that contained the graves of people who, in death, were thought to be actual vampires. Standing at those sites provided a somber perspective on how real these beliefs once were. I was also able to view some of Bram Stoker's original notes for his 1897 novel, *Dracula*. It was a brilliant look into how the author composed what would become one of the most influential vampire works of all time.

Whatever the truth behind those vampire killing kits is, they serve as a testament to the impact that vampires have had on our culture. Also, as far as I'm concerned, they're just plain cool. Sometime after that trip to New York, I visited Los Angeles. While there, I made it a point to stop by the Ripley's in Hollywood—they have a kit too, and I wasn't about to miss it.

With all that said, my hope is that this book sheds some new light on an old monster. We've gotten used to our vampires dwelling quite safely inside books and movies. It's easy to forget that there were times when people lived in very real fear of these creatures. That tradition is what laid the foundation for our big-budget bloodsuckers of today. There's a rich and varied history to explore. Enjoy . . . and keep some garlic with you, just in case.

Endnotes

1. Otelo, "Vampires Killing Essentials," *Ripley's Believe It or Not!*, March 13, 2015. www.ripleys.com/weird-news/vampire-killing-kit/;
Otelo, "Vampire Killing Kits with Charles & Allie," *Ripley's Believe It or Not!*, September 30, 2015. www.ripleys.com/weird-news/vampire-killing-kits.
2. Jonathan Ferguson, "History at Stake! The Story behind Vampire Slaying Kits," *British Library English and Drama Blog*, November 14, 2014. http://blogs.bl.uk/english-and-drama/2014/11/history-at-stake-vampire-slaying-at-the-british-library.html.

1

What Is a ampire?

When using the term "vampire," what exactly do we mean?

Most people could easily come up with a loose definition of what a vampire is based on the pop culture creature that's been featured in so many TV shows, movies, books, and so on. Truth be told, the question can be a pretty easy one when purely looking at modern media. Different writers will often put their own spin on the undead antagonist, or protagonist as the case may be, but it's usually pretty clear on what it means to be a vampire in these settings.

This question starts to get murky when we turn to mythology and folklore. Many cultures have beliefs in creatures that have similarities to what we would recognize as a vampire. Take, for example, the *penanggalan* of Malaysia. One version of the tale states that this being is a woman who, through dark magic, is able to remove her head from her body. The head, with the attached intestines dangling beneath, has the ability to fly. It will suck the blood of its victims, causing death, and usually targets women giving birth. Thorns and a type of thistle known as jeruju would be used to ward off this deadly head, as the creature may snag its entrails on them. The head can later reattach to its body, but not before soaking its intestines in vinegar to reduce swelling.[1]

So, is the *penanggalan* a vampire? It certainly sucks blood, and the use of jeruju might be considered reminiscent of the use of garlic or other plants in vampire tales. However, this is a living person transforming herself through magic, not a deceased person rising from the dead. In my opinion, that's an important distinction to make. Of course, regardless of how you classify it, I think we can all agree that the imagery of the *penanggalan* is truly terrifying!

For another example, let's look at the *empusa* of ancient Greece. It is interesting to note that the Greek word "empusa" is sometimes translated into English as "vampire." These creatures are demons that have the ability to change their shape.[2] In one story, an *empusa* appears as a beautiful, wealthy woman and beguiles a young man named Menippus. His friend, a famous philosopher named Apollonius, understands the woman's true nature and tries to warn him. Unfortunately, Menippus refuses to believe and instead decides to marry her. On the day of the wedding, Apollonius confronts the bride. Although she feigns offense, the truth is revealed—the gold cups and silver, as well as all the servants present, are shown to be illusions. She then confesses that her plan was to devour the young man, and makes special mention of desiring blood.[3]

How do we feel about the *empusa*? Is it a vampire? It certainly has a taste for blood, and its shape-changing abilities might remind us of some vampire stories. However, the *empusa* is not an undead human—rather, it is a distinct, nonhuman creature. Also, its powers of illusion seem to go beyond what we would expect from a vampire. So, even with the similarities, classifying it could be tricky.

The *pananggalan* and *empusa* are just two examples of the great variety of vampire-like creatures that exist throughout the world in mythology and folklore. For the purpose of this book, I would like to narrow down the definition of what a vampire is. Therefore, I will mainly concern myself with beings that

- ✦ are the undead corpses of once-living people,
- ✦ are harming the living in some way, and
- ✦ are killed via taking action against the corpse itself.

Ultimately, I will consider vampires to be dead bodies that are maintaining some aspect of their vitality, often to the detriment of the living. Regardless of what term is actually used (whether it's vampire, revenant, or some other name), if they meet the above criteria, they're fair game for consideration. I also want to mention that not everyone may agree with this approach, and other authors may cast a wider or narrower net. I may even deviate a bit when there's something interesting, or just creepy, to talk about. Overall, though, having these rules will help us nail down, or stake down, traditional vampire beliefs.

Endnotes

1. Walter William Skeat, *Malay Magic: Being an Introduction to the Folklore and Popular Religion of the Malay Peninsula* (London: MacMillan, 1900), 328–329. https://books.google.com/books?id=AOc-AAAAYAAJ.
2. Montague Summers, *The Vampire in Europe (*New Hyde Park, NY: University Books, 1961; reprinted as *The Vampire in Lore and Legend* [Mineola, NY: Dover, 2013]), 3.
3. Philostratus, *The Life of Appolonius of Tyana: The Epistles of Apollonius and the Treatise of Eusebius*, vol. 1, trans. F. C. Conybeare (London: William Heinemann, 1912), 403–409. https://books.google.com/books?id=nzghyc2nJbMC.

2

Blood Drinking

To get things started, let's dive right in and talk about one of the most defining characteristics of the popular vampire: its consumption of blood. Most any work of fiction, past or present, book or TV show, will feature this key element. The tone of this act can be portrayed in a variety of ways: seductive, vicious, or perhaps even perfunctory. It all depends on the nature of the story being told. The vampires of popular media can be lovers, brutal killers, or both. But regardless of how they get it, fresh blood is essential for all of them.

With this emphasis on the red stuff in fiction, what about the folklore? Well, let's look at one of the most famous accounts of a supposed vampire: the case of Peter Plogojowitz, who died in the village of Kisilova, Serbia, in 1725. Ten weeks after his death, something disturbing started happening—villagers began dying of an illness that appeared only twenty-four hours beforehand. On their deathbeds, these people claimed that Plogojowitz came to them while they were asleep. These victims stated that they were strangled by the dead man as he lay on top of them. Ultimately, nine villagers of varying ages died within the span of a single week. Additionally, Plogojowitz's widow fled the village after claiming that her husband had returned, requesting his shoes.[1]

The people ultimately went to the Imperial Provisor (a government official), requesting that he and a parish priest be present when they opened the grave of Plogojowitz. Their plan was to inspect the corpse for signs of vampirism. The official at first tried to dissuade the townsfolk from doing anything until a higher authority could grant permission. However, he was eventually compelled to acquiesce, as the people were so scared they were willing to entirely abandon the village. So, the official and the priest went to Kisilova and examined the recently exhumed body of Peter Plogojowitz. Although we'll get into all the particulars of what they saw and did in the next chapters, one detail is highly relevant for this discussion: Upon viewing the corpse, the onlookers saw that its mouth contained fresh blood. They took this as evidence that Plogojowitz had sucked this blood from his victims.[2]

A separate account, which has been interpreted as the same case,[3] gives the dead man's age as sixty-two. It goes on to say that after having been buried for three days, he made a nighttime visit to his son and requested some food. Once having eaten what was provided, the dead man left. The following day, the son informed his neighbors of what happened, and that night passed without incident. However, on the next night, the son again received a visitation from his hungry father. This time no one knew what happened, but the son is found in bed the next morning, no longer alive.[4]

This whole blood-sucking affair was quite newsworthy at the time. The Imperial Provisor's report was published in the Austrian newspaper *Wienerisches Diarium* on July 21, 1725. If you look at the text, which was written in German, you'll see that the word used for these undead menaces is "Vampyri."[5]

So, there you have it—a reported instance of a vampire sucking blood. This isn't the only tale to feature this trait, but it's a well-documented one and gives us a great example of how blood consumption is present in folkloric beliefs. But let's consider this mouth blood in more detail. It seems to have convinced the villagers as to what the vampire's beverage of choice was. So did they really see this, or is it simply the product of hysteria? Well, in Paul Barber's book *Vampires, Burial and Death: Folklore and Reality*, he explains that

blood around the mouth, which was believed to be one of the signs of a vampire, can actually be a normal part of the body's decomposition process.

Blood can pool depending on body position, and it can actually get pushed to the mouth due to a buildup of gases.[6] Forensic biologist Dr. Mark Benecke, when discussing vampire beliefs, also mentions that decomposition fluid can naturally appear around the mouth.[7]

Of course, based on what the victims reported, sucking blood wasn't this vampire's sole activity. The assertion that he lay on top of people and strangled them may seem like a peculiar detail, especially when we think of vampires from the movies. It just doesn't seem like something Dracula would do. However, this phenomenon can also be found in other stories, and not just in eastern Europe. For example, the chronicler William of Newburgh (1136–1198) gives an account of a dead man from the county of Buckingham, England, who terrorized his widow by visiting her in the night and placing the substantial weight of his body on top of her. However, if she stayed awake and was kept company, he would not appear. Although this dead man ended up doing the same thing to others, the story never mentions anyone actually dying from his assaults.[8] This English account actually sounds quite similar to what is experienced by those who have a condition known today as sleep paralysis. In it, sufferers wake up during the REM stage of sleep. When this happens, they are unable to move and can experience hallucinations caused by their dreaming state. Some people have actually felt as if something sinister was holding them down.[9]

And yet, other beliefs have vampires taking a much less hands-on approach to things. The Kashubians (an ethnic group from Poland) believed that the *vieszcy* would gnaw on its hands and feet while remaining in the grave. Doing this would somehow cause sickness and death in its family and neighbors. Only when this vampire had run out of its own flesh would it leave the grave to terrorize and suck the blood of the living.[10] Also, one description of the Greek *vrykolakas* has it that these undead people are so terrifying that just seeing one would kill the observer. Given this, the creature would be blamed if a rash of unexpected deaths occurred without any accompanying illness.[11]

Vampires and illness often go hand in hand, though. For example, during an 1873 cholera outbreak in a region of Ukraine, it was believed that the root of the problem was an undead corpse.[12] In eighteenth- and nineteenth-century New England, there were various instances where people believed that the dead were causing their relatives to become ill and die of consumption. Of course, the real cause was tuberculosis bacteria.[13]

Besides fearing for their lives, some vampire victims had to fear for their property. Such is the case in an account from French botanist Joseph Pitton de Tournefort. While he was visiting the Greek island of Mykonos in the year 1700, a *vrykolakas* was believed to be present in the very town that Tournefort and his companions were staying in. Thankfully, this one didn't cause immediate death to those who saw it, but it was reported to have assaulted people. Interestingly, villagers also blamed the vampire for causing all kinds of mischief and vandalism, such as putting out lamps, tearing clothes, banging windows, breaking down doors, and even drinking their wine! Although it seemed clear to Tournefort that some "vagabonds" were responsible (and they were even briefly jailed), the villagers had their minds set that a *vrykolakas* was to blame.[14]

Although blood drinking has become inextricably linked with the modern notion of a vampire, the variety of examples discussed in this chapter shows how folklore can be much more nuanced. Sucking blood is just one way in which the dead could terrorize their family and former neighbors. You may also be surprised to learn that on occasion, it wasn't just the vampires who were consuming blood. In the late seventeenth century, one publication asserted that some people in Poland and Russia would eat bread made from the blood of a vampire, believing that it would serve as a means of protection against the creature.[15] This gruesome role reversal illustrates how familiar themes can take unexpected turns in vampire folklore.

-◄◄◄◆►►►-

Endnotes

1. Paul Barber, *Vampires, Burial and Death: Folklore and Reality* (New Haven, CT: Yale University Press, 2010), 5–6.
2. Ibid.
3. Summers, *The Vampire in Lore and Legend*, 149.
4. Marquis D'Argens, *The Jewish Spy: Being a Philosophical, Historical, and Critical Correspondence, by Letters, Which Lately Passed between Certain Jews in Turkey, Italy, France, &c.*, vol. 4, 3rd ed. (London: A. Millar, 1766), 122–123. https://books.google.com/books?id=vXEYAAAAYAAJ.
5. "Copia eines Schreibens aus dem Gradisker District in Ungarn," *Wienerisches Diarium* (Vienna, Austria), July 21, 1725. http://anno.onb.ac.at/cgi-content/anno?aid=wrz&datum=17250721&zoom=33.
6. Barber, *Vampires, Burial and Death*, 115.
7. Diana Zaslaw, dir., *Vampire Secrets*, DVD (New York: A&E Television Networks, 2006).
8. William of Newburgh, *The History of William of Newburgh: The Chronicles of Robert de Monte*, in *The Church Historians of England*, trans. Joseph Stevenson, vol. 4, pt. 2 (London: Seeleys, 1856), 656–657. https://books.google.com/books?id=dBQ5AQAAMAAJ.
9. David Cox, "Vampires, Ghosts, and Demons: The Nightmare of Sleep Paralysis," *The Guardian*, October 30, 2015. www.theguardian.com/science/blog/2015/oct/30/vampires-ghosts-and-demons-the-nightmare-of-sleep-paralysis.
10. W. R. S. Ralston, *Russian Folk-Tales* (New York: R. Worthington, 1880), 325. https://books.google.com/books?id=LTMYAAAAYAAJ.
11. Summers, *The Vampire in Lore and Legend*, 224.
12. "Grabesschändung hilft gegen Cholera," *Neues Wiener Abendblatt* (Vienna, Austria), 213 (August 4, 1873), in *Neues Wiener Tagblatt 1873*. https://books.google.com/books?id=5ZM396nN_gIC.
13. Nickolette Patrick, "Bacteria with Fangs," *Northeastern Spotlight* 4, no. 3 (Fall 2009): 6–7. http://globaltb.njms.rutgers.edu/downloads/products/RTMCCSpotlight-Fall2009.pdf.
14. Joseph Pitton de Tournefort, *A Voyage into the Levant*, vol. 1 (London: D. Midwinter, 1741), 142–147. https://books.google.com/books?id=Bgk-AQAAMAAJ.
15. Augustine Calmet, *The Phantom World: The History and Philosophy of Spirits, Apparitions, &c. &c.*, vol. 2, trans. Henry Christmas (Philadelphia: A. Hart, 1850), 273. https://books.google.com/books?id=Z1GqcY9ow3QC.

3

adaberous

The appearance of modern fictional vampires can certainly vary. They can be anywhere from quite monstrous to very attractive—sometimes changing between both right in front of the camera. However, if we had to describe the stereotypical vampire, the sort that we might see in Halloween ads, what comes to mind for this creature's build and complexion? I'm guessing that many people would say that vampires are usually depicted as being thin and pale—one might say cadaverous.

This is definitely not a new trend in fiction. You even find these traits in the title character of Bram Stoker's 1897 novel, *Dracula*. And it certainly seems to make sense, right? Vampires, being undead, would appear to be likely candidates for having a deathly pallor. Plus, being nocturnal, they never have the opportunity to get a healthy tan. Paleness is also a symptom of anemia (a condition that can be brought about by loss of blood), so there's an interesting parallel there. In regard to their skinny physique, that could play to their attractiveness or be more akin to a deathlike wasting away, depending on the story. Then again, maybe it's just that a blood-based diet keeps their weight down. But does this trend extend into traditional vampire beliefs? Let's return to the official account of Peter Plogojowitz to help answer this.

When the villagers opened the coffin of this suspected vampire, the sight of Plogojowitz's corpse provided what they believed to be proof of his unnatural state. We've already discussed the blood in his mouth, but there was more evidence than that. His corpse, apart from the nose, had apparently not decomposed and there was no foul smell. Rather, his body was still intact. Old skin had peeled to reveal fresh skin beneath, and new fingernails had grown, replacing the old ones that had fallen off. His hair and beard were also longer.[1] In the other version of this tale that I referenced earlier, it mentions that his eyes were open and he was even breathing![2]

So, rather than appearing pale and deathly, the emphasis here was how alive the corpse seemed. Vampires appearing like regular, living people certainly have their place in modern fiction, so this aspect of the Plogojowitz tale may not seem to be especially surprising. However, folklore has more to offer on this topic.

In another tale from William of Newburgh, the corpse of a recently deceased man began terrorizing the inhabitants of an English town located near Anantis Castle. Although the people avoided being physically attacked by remaining indoors at night, the dead man's breath ended up contaminating the air and thus caused a plague. Many townsfolk died or left out of fear. Ultimately, two brothers decided to dig up the corpse and dispatch it in order to save themselves and avenge their father's death. When they unearthed the dead man, his appearance was striking. His body was substantially bloated and his face appeared swollen and flush. There's one other detail you may also find interesting. When the corpse was pierced, a great amount of blood issued forth.[3] In the Latin version of this tale, this last detail caused the dead man to be referred to as a *sanguisuga*,[4] a term that can be translated as "leech" or "bloodsucker."

I think we can all agree that an overweight, red-faced vampire would seem pretty unusual to us based on what we see on TV and in the movies. However, these traits are actually quite common in folklore and are in no way limited to medieval England. For example, the Greek *vrykolakas* has been described as having a very swollen body, resulting in joints that can barely bend and skin so taught that striking it makes the sound of a drum.[5] Shifting our focus north, there is a tale set in early-nineteenth-century Russia that involves the vampire of a deceased provincial governor. When he was dug up in order to end his nighttime assaults on his widow, he was found "gorged with blood, and with red cheeks and lips."[6] As a final example, there's a 1733 discussion of Serbian vampire beliefs that states that these beings are "turgid and full of Blood." It also mentions their faces "are fresh and ruddy."[7] If you design your next Halloween costume based on this type of vampire, it's doubtful that many people will know what you're supposed to be.

In an interesting sidenote, fiction is not completely devoid of this type of portrayal. Although Count Dracula is often described as pale and thin in the novel, he is capable of taking on a more folkloric appearance as well. When the captive Jonathan Harker finds Dracula dormant after having fed, he states that the count appears "gorged with blood" and also remarks on his "bloated face."[8]

In the previous chapter, it was mentioned that blood (or something resembling it) around the mouth is actually a normal part of the decomposition process. You may be surprised to learn that many of the other vampiric indicators can naturally occur as well. Paul Barber asserts that many vampire beliefs in folklore really just stem from a misunderstanding of what was seen when a corpse was exhumed.[9] His fascinating theory has certainly gained traction and has been referenced in other vampire-related works.[10] I'll additionally note that Dr. Mark Benecke has also made links between various decomposition effects and vampires.[11]

Let's take a quick look at what can happen to the regular dead, rather than the undead. First of all, the skin can indeed take on a reddish hue due to various factors affecting the blood. Also, as the outer layer of skin peels, the red-colored layer beneath becomes visible. Hair and nails can appear to have grown due to the skin receding and, if the fingernails have fallen off, the nail beds could be mistaken as new nails. In regard to the vampire's bloated or gorged appearance, the body can in fact swell due to a buildup of gases. Additionally, liquid blood should not necessarily be surprising as coagulation can be temporary in certain situations.[12] Even from a modern perspective, it's quite easy to see how some of this could shock and surprise onlookers.

When we take a step back, it actually makes a lot of sense that the folkloric vampire is rarely ever thin and pale. Those are characteristics that we associate, rightly or wrongly, with a normal corpse—but the vampire, by its very definition, is abnormal. Its unnatural state is reflected in its appearance, whether it's an apparent lack of decay or a bloated transformation. If the villagers had exhumed a suspected vampire only to find a pale and withered body in the ground, they may have started digging elsewhere.

Of course, when talking in terms of beliefs in the supernatural, there are no absolutes. If you're wondering if there are any references out there to a thin and pale folkloric vampire, I do have one I'd like to briefly share. In 1872, a "slim" and "cadaverous" *vrykolakas* was believed to be terrorizing the town of Adrianople, Turkey. It didn't apparently do much harm aside from lurking around houses and making noises. The religious authorities couldn't dispel this vampire, and ultimately a sorcerer was paid to travel to the town. Once he arrived, the monster ceased to be a problem. The author who recounted the tale was of the opinion that the townsfolk had simply been swindled.[13]

So, if thin, pale vampires don't have a strong presence in folklore, what *did* popularize this idea? When did vampires change their image so drastically? I did mention *Dracula* earlier, so you may be wondering if that novel first started the trend. Well, we actually need to go a little further back, to 1819. On April 1 of that year, a short story titled "The Vampyre: A Tale by Lord Byron" was published in the *New Monthly Magazine*. It revolved around Aubrey, a young man whose life ended up taking a traumatic and dire turn due to his acquaintance with the sinister vampire Lord Ruthven. The two met in London society and set out together to travel Europe. However, Aubrey soon noticed that his friend seemed to have a ruinous effect on those he appeared to help. As things progressed, Aubrey observed firsthand Ruthven's regenerative powers as well as his murderous intent. When the story describes the appearance of this vampire, it states, "In spite of the deadly hue of his face, which never gained a warmer tint, either from the blush of modesty, or from the strong emotion of passion, though its form and outline were beautiful."[14] Now, this certainly sounds like something we'd find in modern fiction.

As seen in the title, the initial publication was attributed to the famous poet Lord Byron. However, it turned out that this was incorrect. It was actually written by Byron's former doctor and traveling companion, John Polidori. Although both men separately tried to set the record straight, claims still continued that it was Byron's. Interestingly, the poet was not completely unconnected from the story. Polidori based "The Vampyre" on an abandoned tale that Byron had come up with one evening as part of a ghost story contest with some friends (another work that found its start that same evening was *Frankenstein* by Mary Shelley!). Furthermore, some may argue that Polidori actually based the title character on Byron, as there was often conflict between the two men. Of course, even though Byron didn't write it, his name likely helped popularize "The Vampyre," and the work ultimately was adapted into various plays and operas. Although most moviegoers may not be familiar with this tale, its influence can undoubtedly be seen in the attractive, suave, and mysterious vampires we know today.

Another relevant work that helped define the vampire's look was *Varney the Vampire; or, The Feast of Blood*. It began life as a popular weekly serial, which was then compiled into a more than 800-page novel and published in 1847. This actually makes it the first vampire novel written in English (keeping in mind that Polidori's "The Vampyre" was a short story). The authorship of this work has been the subject of some debate, but it seems that the likely candidate is James Malcolm Rymer.[15] The story itself is about a vampire named Sir Francis Varney, and it follows his long and various exploits. So what did Varney look like? He is described as "tall and gaunt" and "perfectly white—perfectly bloodless."[16] Interestingly, just like Dracula, Varney's countenance changes after feeding—his face being described as "hideously flushed with colour."[17]

Ultimately, it seems that the thin, pale vampire we're familiar with today is actually a product of nineteenth-century literature. It's during this period that the vampire takes on the expected characteristics of death, or perhaps anemia.

The traditional ruddiness, once so common in folklore, takes a backseat, perhaps only being seen after the vampire has devoured the blood of the living. This was an important evolutionary step toward today's conceptions of what it means to be a vampire.

—«‹•›»—

Endnotes

1. Barber, *Vampires, Burial and Death*, 6.
2. D'Argens, *The Jewish Spy*, 123.
3. Newburgh, *The History of William of Newburgh*, 660–661.
4. Willelmi Parvi de Newburgh, *Historia Rerum Anglicarum*, vol. 2 (London: Sumptibus Societatis, 1856), 190. https://books.google.com/books?id=tOY9AAAAcAAJ.
5. Henry Newpher Bowman, *The Crimes of the Oedipodean Cycle* (Boston: Richard G. Badger, 1918), 47. https://books.google.com/books?id=iLhHAAAAIAAJ.
6. H. P. Blavatsky, *Isis Unveiled: A Master-Key to the Mysteries of Ancient and Modern Science and Theology*, vol. 1, 6th ed. (New York: J. W. Bouton, 1892), 454–455. https://books.google.com/books?id=ca70UR08tOoC.
7. "The Travels of Three English Gentlemen, from Venice to Hamburgh, Being the Grand Tour of Germany, in the Year 1734," in *The Harleian Miscellany; or, a Collection of Scarce, Curious, and Entertaining Pamphlets and Tracts, as Well in Manuscript as in Print, Found in the Late Earl of Oxford's Library, Interspersed with Historical, Political, and Critical Notes*, vol. 4 (London: T. Osborne, 1745), 358. https://books.google.com/books?id=X11UAAAAcAAJ.
8. Bram Stoker, *Dracula*, 6th ed. (Westminster, UK: Archibald Constable, 1899), 52. https://books.google.com/books?id=hhBEAQAAMAAJ.
9. Barber, *Vampires, Burial and Death*, 13.
10. Specifically:
Michael E. Bell, *Food for the Dead: On the Trail of New England's Vampires* (New York: Carroll & Graff, 2001), 233;
J. Gordon Melton, *The Vampire Book: The Encyclopedia of the Undead*, 3rd ed. (Detroit: Visible Ink, 2011), 244.
11. Zaslaw, *Vampire Secrets*, DVD; "The Restless Dead: Vampires and Decomposition," *Bizarre Magazine*, May–June 1997, 60–61, posted at Dr. Mark Benecke: International Forensic Research & Consulting, August 21, 2015. http://home.benecke.com/publications/the-restless-dead-vampires-and-decomposition.
12. Barber, *Vampires, Burial and Death*, 105, 109, 114–117, 119, 161. Some examples also discussed in "The Restless Dead: Vampires and Decomposition."
13. Mrs. John Elijah Blunt, *The People of Turkey: Twenty Years' Residence among Bulgarians, Greeks, Albanians, Turks, and Armenians*, vol. 2 (London: John Murray, 1878), 225–226. https://books.google.com/books?id=sZj2tM-iUlUC.
14. "The Vampyre; A Tale by Lord Byron," *New Monthly Magazine* 1, no. 63 (April 1, 1819), reprinted in *New Monthly Magazine and Universal Register*, vol. 11 (London: Henry Colburn, 1819), 196. https://books.google.com/books?id=VCQ8AQAAMAAJ.
15. Here are some of the various discussions regarding authorship: Montague Summers, *The Vampire: His Kith and Kin* (New York: E. P. Dutton, 1929; reprinted as *Vampires and Vampirism* [Mineola, NY: Dover, 2005]), x; Melton, *The Vampire Book*, 598–599; Leslie S. Klinger, "The Context of Dracula," in Bram Stoker, *The New Annotated Dracula*, ed. Leslie S. Klinger (New York: W. W. Norton, 2008), xix–xix.
16. James Malcolm Rymer or Thomas Preskett Prest, *Varney the Vampire; or, The Feast of Blood* (London: E. Lloyd, 1847), chapter 1, paragraphs 15 and 21. www.gutenberg.org/ebooks/14833.
17. Rymer or Prest, *Varney the Vampire*, chapter 2, paragraph 61.

4

take through
the Heart

A wooden stake and mallet are ubiquitous tools for most fictional vampire hunters. After gaining access to the resting place of this undead creature, the intrepid hero will then have the opportunity to drive a stake right through the very heart of the monster while it sleeps. As the stake goes in, the vampire will likely react in a memorable (and possibly gory) way before finally becoming a true corpse. It's a scene that's been interpreted in a variety of ways in many works. With this well-established trend in mind, let's now finish the account of Peter Plogojowitz to find out the true beliefs.

According to the report, once the villagers had concluded that Plogojowitz was a vampire, they did indeed prepare a stake. It was then driven into the dead man's heart and, upon doing so, a great amount of blood (which was believed to be fresh) came out of his chest, ears, and mouth. As a final step, the corpse of Peter Plogojowitz was burned until it was ashes.[1]

No doubt the efficacy of a stake through the heart was certainly a real belief, and staking appears in other tales as well. For example, in the previous chapter, I briefly mentioned a story regarding the vampire of a deceased Russian governor who made nightly assaults upon his widow. In order to finally stop him, his body was exhumed and a stake of oak was driven though his heart. Upon doing so, blood shot into the air and the vampire groaned. An archbishop then performed an exorcism, and the body was once again buried.[2]

Just between these two tales, we're already seeing a bit of variation. After staking, one vampire is burned while the other is reburied after a ritual. It's also interesting to note that the second story specifically mentions that the stake was made of oak. Was the wood important? Was burning the corpse essential? Was the staking even necessary if other actions were performed? Let's delve deeper and try to answer these questions.

Let's first discuss the material a stake is made of. You may be surprised to learn that a number of authors have discussed which woods were preferred in different parts of Europe. Montague Summers, who published two books on vampires in the 1920s, informs us that aspen and whitethorn were used in the Slavic tradition,[3] while aspen and maple stakes were favored in Russia. He also mentions hawthorn and whitethorn being used more generally.[4] Dudley Wright, in his 1924 book on vampires, also comments on the popularity of whitethorn and adds that ash was used in Bukowina.[5] Professor T. P. Vukanović, in his 1958 article on the vampire beliefs of the Romani, informs us that stakes were cut from hawthorn, wild rose, and juniper trees.[6] Additionally, a 1922 encyclopedia on religion states that hawthorn and blackthorn were used in Serbia.[7] (Just to clarify a few of these thorny plants: Whitethorn is another name for hawthorn, while blackthorn is a similar but separate plant—and, as you would guess, they do all have thorns.) While this list is certainly not exhaustive, it nicely demonstrates the variety of customs that vampire researchers have encountered.

So, why exactly did the wood matter? Montague Summers points out that some wood varieties have religious significance. For example, there was a tradition that the cross on which Jesus was crucified was made of aspen. Additionally, whitethorn was believed to have been used for Christ's Crown of

Thorns.[8] A different source mentions a belief in the Crown being made of blackthorn.[9] If these trees did hold special meaning for those people living in fear of vampires, it certainly seems reasonable that they would utilize the wood to combat the supernatural. Of course, one also wonders if some woods were favored simply due to their availability in the region.

As with other vampire-related beliefs, you will start to find differences as you delve deeper—such as the Romani practices of staking the stomach or forehead, rather than the chest.[10] You'll also find that in some traditions, the instrument wasn't even made of wood. For example, piercing the heart with a red-hot iron was the approach in Bulgaria. In one Transylvanian town, the tradition was to stick iron forks into the eyes as well as the heart/chest before reburying the corpse face down.

In a somewhat less dramatic approach, the inhabitants of one area of Romania would just put a needle into the heart.

Interestingly, sometimes the corpse didn't even have to be actively staked. Rather, distaffs (which are wooden, stake-like tools used in spinning yarn) would be driven into the grave. If the corpse arose as a vampire, it would stake itself![11] Lastly, I'll mention a very unique Russian tradition, which states that the stake must be driven into the vampire with a single blow. If a second swing is applied, the vampire will be revived.[12]

Perhaps a bigger question relates to the rationale behind this practice. Why was staking a vampire believed to stop it? Some tales provide an extra detail that helps us form a clearer picture. Here's how H. P. Blavatsky describes the approach that locals used to deal with the undead Russian governor: "The archbishop then resolved, as a last expedient, to resort to the time-honored plan of exhuming the body, and pinning it to the earth with an oaken stake driven through his heart."[13] Notice it wasn't just about impaling the heart; they also wanted to affix the body to the ground. Dom Calmet, in his influential eighteenth-century work analyzing vampire beliefs, includes the following about the practice in northern Europe: "At other times they thrust a stake through the body and thus fixed them to the ground."[14] With this detail in mind, the stake takes on a less magical role and gains a much more practical one. Essentially, the stake could immobilize the vampire, physically preventing it from rising out of the grave. This concept especially makes sense when we realize that there was a time when not all corpses were buried in coffins.

Staking may also be related to the belief that a vampire's body became bloated (as discussed in the previous chapter). In Serbia and Bulgaria, besides staking the supposed vampire through the heart, they would also drive a nail into the back of its neck. The rationale was that these acts would prevent the devil from causing the body to swell, and thus the corpse would not be animated as a vampire.[15]

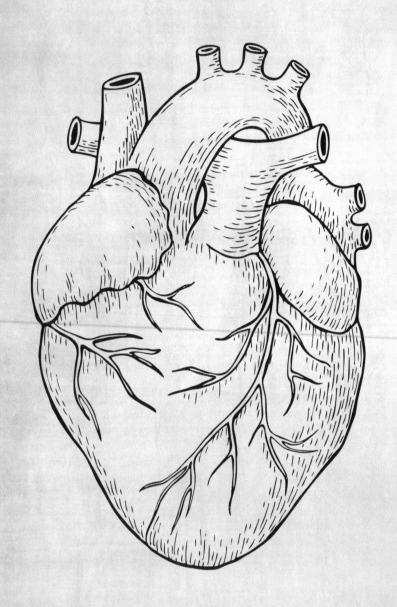

Pinning and bloating aside, one could argue that another possible purpose for staking a vampire was simply to destroy the heart itself. After all, the heart is a vital, blood-related organ, and it has been connected to the soul going all the way back to ancient Egypt. This additional explanation starts to seem even more likely when you realize that in certain vampire accounts, the hearts were specifically destroyed in ways other than staking.

For example, one account describes how, in the village of Cuşmir, Romania, in the late nineteenth century, the relatives of a deceased, disabled bachelor started becoming sick and dying. Each victim would claim that one of their legs was withering. Suspicion fell on the bachelor, and his body was exhumed. The villagers found that he had shifted into the corner of the grave, and his skin had become red.

The people cut out his heart and liver, which were then burned. The ashes were mixed with water and given to the sick to drink. As the story goes, the victims were then cured. [16]

In a different Romanian tradition, the entire body would be burned, but the heart would be saved for last. When the heart was finally consigned to the flames, people would gather near so that the smoke would envelope them. This act would serve as a protection against evil. [17]

The practice of consuming the ashes or inhaling the smoke of a burning heart may seem quite shocking to the modern reader. It's certainly not something we're used to seeing in movies. However, these traditions are not isolated to eastern Europe. Fascinatingly, both practices were also seen half a world away in New England.

In the American town of Exeter, Rhode Island, in 1892, a young man by the name of Edwin Brown was dying of consumption (tuberculosis). As part of an attempt to save his life, the bodies of his mother and two sisters, all of whom had previously died of the disease, were exhumed. The townspeople were looking to see if fresh blood could be found in any of the hearts. They believed this would be evidence that the deceased was the cause of Edwin's disease. The mother and one sister had both decomposed to the point that they were beyond suspicion. However, the body of Edwin's other sister, Mercy Lena, was well preserved. She had died just a couple months previously at the age of nineteen. Her heart and liver were cut out and, although the blood in the heart was coagulated and the liver contained no blood, Mercy's body was identified as the source of the illness. Both organs were then burned in the cemetery. The resulting ashes were supposedly mixed with water and given as a drink to Edwin. Unfortunately, this grim cure had no effect, and Edwin Brown died not long after. [18]

In a case from Foster, Rhode Island, the body of Nancy Young was exhumed in 1827, shortly after her death from consumption at the age of nineteen. Other members of her family were suffering from the disease, and her remains were burned in an attempt to save them. The family gathered near the flames and inhaled the smoke, hoping that it would serve as a cure. However, the attempt proved ineffective, and more family members passed away.[19]

Beyond the surprising parallel practices involving smoke and ashes, it seems we have also returned to the act of burning the corpse—just as was done in the Peter Plogojowitz case. In many vampire accounts, this seems to be the ultimate way to deal with the threat. For example, in the *vrykolakas* incident observed by Tournefort in 1700, the corpse's heart was removed, religious rituals were performed, and swords were shoved into the grave—but the villagers were finally satisfied only after having burned the body on a pyre.[20] In the case of William of Newburgh's *sanguisuga*, the heart was removed and torn apart, and then the corpse was burned. The account also mentions that the plague brought on by the dead man then ceased, as if the flames had purified the air.[21] This is an interesting point and suggests that some beliefs ascribe a sanitizing effect to the fire. Of course, the physical destruction accomplished by the fire was likely the main reason for its use.

For those thinking that perhaps cremation seems like overkill, let's look at an account that supposedly took place in the village of Blow, near Kadam (in what is now the Czech Republic). In this tale, a deceased shepherd started appearing in the village and calling out to people. Whomever he addressed ended up dying within eight days. To deal with this threat, the villagers dug up the shepherd's grave and staked his body, securing it to the ground. Surprisingly, not only does this fail to kill him, he actually makes fun of the attempt. The shepherd thanked the people for giving him a stick that he can use against dogs! That night, he then went on a more vicious rampage, strangling a number of people. At this point, the corpse was handed over to the executioner to cart it out of the village for burning. The dead man, perhaps knowing what was in store, started wailing and moving his hands and feet. Before being thrown into the flames, the villagers drove a number of stakes through the body. This time, a more expected result was produced: Red blood flows out, and the dead man loudly yells. Once the corpse was finally destroyed in the fire, the "spectre" never troubled the village again.[22]

The account of the Blow vampire certainly contains some memorable details. It's not often that a vampire makes a sarcastic comment after being staked. It's also interesting that this undead shepherd caused death in others simply by calling for them (we'll discuss more about this phenomenon later in the book). Ultimately, for the purpose of this chapter, this story is a great example of how burning, rather than staking, was sometimes seen as the best and most reliable way to kill a vampire.

We've covered a lot of ground, from Europe all the way to the New World. It's clear that staking often plays a vital role in vampire traditions, but it is not omnipresent and sometimes not entirely effective. Regardless of the specifics, it would seem certain that none of these measures would be taken lightly. We must remember that these aren't all just stories—many are well-documented accounts. Even the more fantastic ones likely have some kernel of truth to them. These deeds may seem gruesome, but one can only imagine the fear and desperation felt by those people trying to protect themselves and their loved ones from some misunderstood affliction. It's these cases where the monsters teach us about humanity.

⤙⤙◈⤚⤚

Endnotes

1. Barber, *Vampire, Burial and Death*, 6–7.
2. Blavatsky, *Isis Unveiled*, 454–455.
3. Summers, *The Vampire in Lore and Legend*, 257.
4. Summers, *Vampires and Vampirism*, 203.
5. Dudley Wright, *Vampires and Vampirism,* 2nd ed. (W. Rider & Son: London, 1924, reprinted as *The Book of Vampires* [Mineola, NY: Dover, 2006]), 4–5.
6. T. P. Vukanović, "The Vampire," in *Vampire Lore: From the Writings of Jan Louis Perkowski,* trans. Jan Louis Perkowski (Bloomington, IN: Slavica, 2006), 250.
7. J. A. MacCulloch, "Vampire," in *Encyclopædia of Religion and Ethics,* vol. 12, *Suffering–Zwingli,* ed. James Hastings (New York: Charles Scribner's Sons, 1922), 589–591. https://books.google.com/books?id=UD8TAAAAYAAJ.
8. Summers, *Vampires and Vampirism*, 203.
9. "Hawthorn," in *Chamber's Encyclopædia: A Dictionary of Universal Knowledge,* vol. 5 (London: William and Robert Chambers, 1897) 594. https://books.google.com/books?id=QYJRAAAAYAAJ.
10. Vukanović, "The Vampire," 249–250.
11. Agnes Murgoci, "The Vampire in Roumania," *Folklore* 37, no. 4 (1926), reprinted in Emily Gerard and Agnes Murgoci, *Transylvanian Superstitions* (Scripta Minora, 2013), 53–56.
12. Ralston, *Russian Folk-Tales*, 327–328.
13. Blavatsky, *Isis Unveiled*, 455.
14. Calmet, *The Phantom World*, 282.
15. Murgoci, "The Vampire in Roumania," 56.
16. Ibid., 51.
17. Ibid., 52–53.
18. Bell, *Food for the Dead*, 18–22, 33–34.
19. Ibid., 142.
20. Tournefort, *A Voyage into the Levant*, 143–147.
21. Newburgh, *William of Newburgh, Historia Rerum Anglicarum*, 661.
22. Calmet, *The Phantom World*, 261.

5

ecapitation

If there's time after staking a vampire, and its body didn't crumble into dust or something to that effect, a thorough vampire hunter may also remove the creature's head. A fine example of this occurs in the novel *Dracula* when the heroes must confront the vampiric Lucy Westenra. She had been a dear friend to them in life but had joined the ranks of the undead due to Dracula's assaults. After a stake is driven into Lucy's heart, Dr. Van Helsing and Dr. Seward remain to remove her head. This extra precaution also takes place in the lush 1992 film adaptation, *Bram Stoker's Dracula*. Although decapitation may not be the most popular approach used to kill vampires in fiction, it most certainly has its place.

One can indeed find this practice in the folkloric accounts. However, as in fiction, it isn't necessarily the main method. None of the traditional tales mentioned thus far have incorporated this detail. But that doesn't mean there aren't any out there.

One account supposedly occurred around the year 1715 in Hungary. A soldier was lodging at the home of a peasant and witnessed something very odd while dining with the members of the household. A man, whom the soldier had never seen before, entered the home and sat at the table with them. The soldier noticed that the stranger's presence appeared to frighten everyone there, but the tale does not mention anything being said or done at the time. Then, on the following day, the peasant host was found dead. This prompted the soldier to start asking questions. He was informed that the mysterious dinner guest was actually the peasant's father, who had been dead for ten years. It was this undead visitor who caused the peasant to die. The soldier gave the news of this to his regiment, and, ultimately, the Count de Cabreras (a regimental captain) was called in to investigate. The count, along with some officers, a surgeon, and an auditor, visited the members of the household, and the soldier's story was confirmed. The count then had the father's corpse exhumed so it could be examined. The body looked as if the man had only just died, and his blood appeared fresh. Given this evidence, the count ordered that the corpse's head be cut off and then reburied.[1]

As we can see in the above case, sometimes decapitation is the only step taken. In other instances, it's only part of the process. For example, let's look at a sixteenth-century incident concerning a shoemaker who died in the city of Breslau (in modern-day Poland). Though his family tried to conceal the nature of his death, he had apparently committed suicide, and the townspeople believed that his ghost was tormenting them. Some of the claims were that the man was appearing in people's homes at night, hitting and choking them while they were in bed. On April 18, 1592, the shoemaker's body was exhumed after having been buried for almost seven months. The town magistrates and onlookers saw the expected vampiric qualities—the body was well preserved, with supple limbs and seemingly new skin. There was also a mark on his toe in the shape of a rose, which the people took to be magical in nature. After leaving the corpse out for about six days, the townspeople then buried it under the gallows. They thought this reburial would solve the problem—but to no avail. To finally destroy this "Spectrum," the corpse's head, arms, and legs were cut off, the heart was removed, and everything was burned on a pyre. The ashes were placed in a sack and then thrown into a river.[2]

In the case of this shoemaker, the removal of the head was by no means enough for the townspeople involved. It was merely part of an overall process of mutilating the corpse before burning it to ashes. This kind of corpse destruction certainly seems to tie back to what was discussed in the previous chapter. Given that the townspeople's first attempt to deal with the vampire failed, it's likely they wanted to leave no margin for error in their second try.

While we're on the topic of vampire heads (not something one says often), there are some related traditions worth mentioning. In Germanic regions, there was a belief that the dead could start chewing in their graves. They would consume their burial shrouds and flesh, often making audible grunting noises in the process. This phenomenon was thought to occur most frequently during times of plague.[3] These hungry dead were known as *nachzehrer*, and their actions were believed to cause death in those still alive.[4] To prevent these corpses from eating, a very straightforward technique was sometimes used: A coin and a stone would be placed into the dead person's mouth, thus giving them something to chew on.[5] Other approaches involved placing dirt under the chin or tying a handkerchief around the throat.[6] It seems the idea was that if the *nachzehrer* was unable to chew or swallow, the living would be saved.

If we wanted to isolate the overall approach behind many of these vampire mitigation techniques, it seems to come down to people trying to find ways to physically prevent the vampire from moving. This could be accomplished through introducing some kind of obstacle (such as the stake or coin) or though mutilating the corpse such that it would no longer be capable of venturing forth. These practices emphasize the tactile nature of the vampire. They are not simply ghosts or disembodied spirits, untethered to the physical world. Rather, people believed that the root of the problem was a real corpse lying in a real grave somewhere nearby, and something tangible had to be done to stop it.

⸺⸙⸺

Endnotes

1. Calmet, *The Phantom World*, 262–263.
2. Henry More, *An Antidote against Atheism, or An Appeal to the Naturall Faculties of the Mind of Man, Whether There Be Not a God* (London: J. Flesher, 1655), 208–214. https://books.google.com/books?id=gTdOAAAAcAAJ.
3. Summers, *The Vampire in Lore and Legend*, 178, 196–199.
4. Moncure Daniel Conway, *Demonology and Devil-Lore*, vol. 1 (London: Chatto and Windus, 1879), 52. https://books.google.com/books?id=Ck_OAAAAMAAJ.
5. Calmet, *The Phantom World*, 340; Summers, *The Vampire in Lore and Legend*, 202.
6. Calmet, *The Phantom World*, 340.

6

Fangs

"In particular, by some trick of the light, the canine teeth looked longer and sharper than the rest."[1]

In this line from the novel *Dracula*, Dr. Seward unknowingly observes a key symptom of Lucy Westenra's vampiric transformation. This was certainly no trick of the light. Dr. Seward must later learn what is well known these days—vampires have fangs! In fact, fangs are likely the most iconic feature of the fictional vampire and serve as a prominent visual queue. If you're watching a movie and you see someone with elongated canines, you instantly know what that means.

Given that fangs are practically ubiquitous in fictional portrayals of vampires, they must be present in folklore, right? How could they not be? Well, I have some shocking news: Traditional vampire beliefs do NOT incorporate fangs! In fact, in all the vampire accounts I've referenced in this book thus far, fangs have not been present in any of them.

There are a few accounts that mention the vampire's teeth, but they don't have the characteristic fangs we've come to expect. For example, in a tale set in Ireland some years prior to 1925, a deceased priest was seen walking past the funeral procession that had just buried him. The members of the procession, who were naturally quite afraid, noticed that the priest's teeth were now extremely long.[2] Of course, it should be emphasized that long teeth do not equate to fangs. We must be careful not to let modern expectations influence how we interpret these kinds of details. Elongated teeth are also mentioned in a Polish folktale where a deceased man, referred to as an "Upior," appears at his sister's window one night.[3] In Ukraine, it seems that the focus was on the strength of the vampire's teeth, which were believed to be similar to steel. Using this powerful bite, the creature was able to chew its way out of the grave.[4] For something akin to an actual fang, there was a belief in Poland that the tip of a vampire's tongue ended in a sharp, stinger-like barb.[5]

This lack of fangs has some big implications for another piece of iconic vampire imagery—the two wounds that are normally found on the victim's neck. Clearly, since folkloric vampires don't have fangs, they don't leave those marks. Some accounts, such as the Peter Plogojowitz case, don't mention puncture wounds of any kind, and we are left to wonder how exactly the vampire extracted its victim's blood. In other tales, the vampire's methods are discussed in more detail, and, not surprisingly, beliefs vary on this.

In the tale of the vampiric Russian governor, his widow is found bruised from his assault, and "from a slight puncture on her neck drops of blood were oozing."[6] I wanted to mention this detail, as it seems similar to what we would expect to find in modern fiction. However, only one puncture mark is referenced, not the two that we are used to seeing. One wonders if this particular vampire, like in the Polish tradition, had a barbed tongue.

A single neck wound is also present in a tale that was reported to have come from a military officer named Captain Pokrovsky in 1905. In a Lithuanian village that the captain was visiting, there was a wealthy farmer who started suffering from ill health after marrying his second wife. This man was also heard to cry out in the night. A doctor's examination, arranged by Pokrovsky, determined that the farmer had lost a lot of blood, but the cause was unknown. Additionally, a small wound was discovered on the man's neck. Pokrovsky later learns that the farmer had passed away, and the neck wound had apparently grown in size since it was first observed. The people of the village strongly believed that the farmer was the victim of a vampire. Although his widow was religious, suspicion fell on her, and she quickly departed in order to ensure her safety.[7] This tale is rather unique given that the suspected vampire was a living person rather than a deceased one. Perhaps the populace was conflating vampirism with witchcraft (a notion that will be explored in chapter 20).

Unlike these past two accounts, some tales have vampires ignoring the neck, instead targeting different parts of the victim's body. For example, there is an Armenian legend about a vampire named Dakhanavar who lived in a cavern in the Ultmish Altotem Mountains. He would kill anyone who ventured into the area by sucking blood from their feet. Ultimately, he is tricked by two travelers who place their feet under each other's heads while sleeping. The vampire, seeing what appears to be a person with two heads and no feet, is so perplexed that he leaves the mountains and never returns.[8] The details of this legend certainly stand out, and we're left to wonder why the vampire exclusively targeted the feet of mountain climbers. Certainly there must be less odorous options.

In a Russian tale, a vampire enters a house to find an old man and a youth asleep on a bench. The vampire hits the youth on his back, creating a wound that bleeds profusely. Rather than directly drinking this, the vampire fills a pail with the free-flowing blood. He then consumes the pail's contents and repeats the same procedure on the old man. The next day, both victims are found dead.[9] If you want to add a pail as a prop to your vampire costume next Halloween, I'll get the reference.

Aside from the back and feet, another spot mentioned in folklore is the left side of the chest, where one would feel the beating of the heart. The Kashubs believed that a small wound would be found on that spot when someone was the victim of a *vieszcy*.[10] This spot seems to make some sense. After all, if a vampire wants blood, the heart would be the most direct target.

It appears that legends and folklore have left us with fangless vampires who may not even suck blood from the necks of their victims. Given this, we need to turn our gaze to works of fiction to find the source of this modern vampiric notion. I started this chapter with a quote from *Dracula*, but we don't have Bram Stoker to thank for the vampire's piercing bite. Rather, it seems that the first appearance of a fanged vampire was in *Varney the Vampire; or, The Feast of Blood*, from the 1840s. I referenced this penny dreadful back in chapter 3, and it certainly has made a mark, or two, on the neck of our modern conceptions concerning the undead. Here's part of the very first visual description the reader gets of the title character: "The eyes look like polished tin; the lips are drawn back, and the principal feature next to those dreadful eyes is the teeth—the fearful looking teeth—projecting like those of some wild animal, hideously, glaringly white, and fang-like."[11] If there was any doubt, the later descriptions of the vampire's "large canine looking teeth"[12] and "tusk-like teeth"[13] seem to make things pretty clear. I'll also add that when one of his victims is examined, "two small wounds in the neck"[14] are found. This trope is so common these days, it's hard to imagine how fresh and novel this would have been to Victorian readers.

Later nineteenth-century works of fiction, specifically *Carmilla* by Sheridan Le Fanu in 1872 and *Dracula* by Bram Stoker in 1897, would also incorporate fanged vampires. Fangs then made the jump to the big screen in the 1922 German silent film *Nosferatu, eine Symphonie des Grauens*, in which the vampire had ratlike front fangs (I'll discuss this groundbreaking film in more detail in a later chapter). Interestingly, besides *Nosferatu*, many early vampire films didn't feature fangs. This includes Universal's famous 1931 horror film *Dracula*, starring Bela Lugosi. If you thought this classic, black-and-white movie monster was sporting fangs, you may be surprised to learn that he was not! Thankfully for the modern vampire, fangs started coming back into films in the 1950s, and the rest is history.

Endnotes

1. Stoker, *Dracula*, 162.
2. Summers, *The Vampire in Lore and Legend*, 120–121.
3. Otto Knoop, "Sagen aus Kujawien," *Zeitschrift des Vereins für Volkskunde* 16 (1906), 96. https://books.google.com/books?id=C2QKAAAAIAAJ.
4. Ralston, *Russian Folk-Tales*, 325.
5. S. G. B. St. Clair and Charles A. Brophy, *A Residence in Bulgaria* (London: John Murray, 1869), 51. https://books.google.com/books?id=U5FMAAAAcAAJ.
6. Blavatsky, *Isis Unveiled*, 455.
7. Summers, *The Vampire in Lore and Legend*, 299–300.
8. Baron von Haxthausen, *Transcaucasia: Sketches of the Nations and Races between the Black Sea and the Caspian* (London: Chapman & Hall, 1854), 191–192. https://books.google.com/books?id=Qvs9AAAAcAAJ.
9. W. R. S. Ralston, *The Songs of the Russian People: As Illustrative of Slavonic Mythology and Russian Social Life* (London: Ellis & Green, 1872) 411–412. https://books.google.com/books?id=6EFLAAAAYAAJ.
10. Ralston, *Russian Folk-Tales*, 325.
11. Rymer or Prest, *Varney the Vampire*, chapter 1, paragraph 21.
12. Ibid., chapter 2, paragraph 61.
13. Ibid., chapter 9, paragraph 54.
14. Ibid., chapter 4, paragraph 248.

7

Becoming a ampire

How does one actually become a vampire? In fiction, it usually involves getting bitten by one. Sometimes, it's more a matter that the victim has consumed the vampire's blood. Transformations might be relatively immediate, or they may be a more gradual process. Ultimately, regardless of the particulars, you usually need a vampire to become a vampire. Vampirism is essentially contagious, which some works of fiction particularly emphasize.

So, where do our folkloric vampires come from? Well, to help answer this question, we'll look at a very famous historical account—the case of Arnod Paole. As I review the details, keep an eye out for many of the practices and beliefs we've already discussed in the previous chapters.

Around 1727, in the Serbian village of Medvegia, a soldier named Arnod Paole fell from a hay wagon and died of a broken neck. In life, Paole had often told people about how he had once been victimized by a vampire. In order to rid himself of this monster, Paole ate dirt from the vampire's grave and smeared his face with the creature's blood. Unfortunately, this incident made Paole a likely candidate to become a vampire himself, and about twenty or thirty days after his death, that appeared to be the case. Villagers began saying that Paole was tormenting them, and he was ultimately blamed for the deaths of four people. He was also believed to have sucked the blood from cattle. When the corpse of Arnod Paole was exhumed, the classic vampiric signs were observed. His body was well preserved and blood had flowed out of his mouth, eyes, nose, and ears. Also, old skin and nails had fallen off, revealing what appeared to be new growth. To deal with this apparent vampire, a stake was driven through his heart, causing him to groan and bleed. His body was then burned and the ashes were thrown back into the grave. However, the villager's work was not yet done. Remember that the vampiric Paole was thought to have killed four people. The villagers believed that those victims would become vampires themselves. Therefore, those bodies were also exhumed and suffered the same treatment as Paole.[1]

Interestingly, the story doesn't end there. Five years later, the same village had another, more extreme bout of vampirism. This time seventeen people died within a three-month period. In one specific example given, a girl named Stanacka claimed to have been strangled during the night by the teenaged Milloe, who had already been dead for nine weeks. Stanacka, after experiencing severe chest pain, then passed away herself three days later. This new vampiric outbreak was believed to have been started by Miliza, a sixty-year-old woman who had died after a three-month illness. So, you might be wondering how she suddenly became one of the undead. Well, Miliza had once eaten meat from a sheep that had been attacked by a vampire during the incident five years earlier. This meant that upon her death, she would become a vampire as well.[2] It was a meal with major consequences.

In this second occurrence, the recorded account discusses sixteen bodies that were exhumed and examined. Of them, eleven were found to have vampiric symptoms such as liquid blood, a well-preserved condition, and, in the case of Miliza, weight gain. The five other bodies appeared to have decomposed as expected.

The suspected vampires had their heads cut off and were then burned to ashes. Finally, those ashes were thrown into a river. For the bodies that appeared normal, they were simply reburied.[3]

The details I've summarized above come from Paul Barber's English translation of the official report written by Johannes Flückinger, a medical officer and member of a team of officials sent to investigate the second incident. The original event involving Arnod Paole is simply told to the officials by the villagers, given that it had happened five years earlier.[4] In regard to what the undead were actually called, a 1732 German version of the account uses the term "Vampiren" when describing Arnod Paole and those sharing his condition.[5]

This story caused quite a sensation back in eighteenth-century Europe. It sparked a large public debate on the existence of vampires and what the root cause of this phenomenon was. For the purposes of this chapter, however, it's a fantastic example of how people believed someone could be transformed into a vampire. At the risk of anachronistically applying our modern understanding of disease to this, it seems as if the people viewed vampirism as a sort of infection—one that was spread from the attack of the infected. It could even contaminate the meat supply. Plus, it wasn't necessarily fast acting. In Miliza's case, they seemed to believe that the vampirism was lying dormant inside her, only to present itself once she died five years later (of a possibly unrelated illness).

Of course, the case of Arnod Paole is an extreme example. Other accounts don't often involve this level of vampire slaying. For example, although Peter Plogojowitz was believed to have caused the deaths of a number of people, the official report doesn't mention any other villagers being exhumed besides Plogjowitz.[6] A secondary source for that story does mention that the supposed victims were inspected for indications of vampirism, but none exhibited any signs.[7]

So, it looks like the account of Arnod Paole nicely supports our modern notions of vampires creating other vampires. However, I would certainly be remiss if I simply ended the chapter here. You may be surprised to learn that there are a bunch of ways to become a vampire in folklore, and many don't even require the intervention of a preexisting bloodsucker! Here's a selection of Romanian beliefs regarding who's at risk of joining the ranks of the undead:[8]

- Those who were evil in life
- Women who practiced dark magic
- Those who lied to get money
- Children who died before being baptized
- Those who committed suicide
- Those whose mothers didn't eat salt during pregnancy
- Those born with a caul (a piece of amniotic membrane covering the head)
- Corpses that a cat has jumped over
- Corpses that a man has stepped over
- Corpses that a man's shadow has fallen upon
- The seventh son or daughter
- Those who are simply fated to be vampires

Yikes, right? The rules certainly get a lot looser in folklore. Plus, this is just one place. The criteria can shift depending on where you're looking. For example, some Romani traditions held that various animals, not just cats, could create a vampire by jumping over a corpse.[9] In Russia, a bird flying over the body also had the same result.[10] Greece shared the belief that an evildoer could become a *vrykolakas*, but it was especially likely to happen if the person had been excommunicated.[11] Murder victims who hadn't been avenged were also potential candidates.[12]

Once we separate ourselves from the modern notion that vampires can only be created by other vampires, some of these more varied beliefs don't actually seem that surprising. Evil deeds, murders, and suicides can certainly be found in modern ghost stories. If those kinds of events can result in ghosts, maybe it's not such a stretch that they can result in vampires too.

However, many of the other risk factors are not even close to what we're used to. One in particular is the animal jumping over the corpse, which I would like to delve a little deeper into. It is curious as to why this act would transform a normal dead body into a vampire. One wonders if the animal somehow imbues vitality into the corpse, or perhaps it is some kind of desecration that must be avenged. Well, one Romani tradition does provide an explanation: It was believed that when a cat or hen jumped over a corpse, it would split the dead person's soul in two, and that would result in a vampire. I realize that this seems to raise more questions than it answers, but a different Romani tradition helps put this into perspective. In this other belief, there is a concept of everyone having two souls—one that always remains within us and one that wanders while we sleep. Death occurs when the stationary soul leaves the body. If this happens while the wandering soul is away, the person will become a vampire. If both souls depart together, the vampiric condition is avoided.[13] Perhaps, when an animal splits the soul, one part remains (just like the wandering soul), and this animates the dead body.

Ultimately, the causes of vampirism leave us with a lot of questions. The roots of these risk factors are obscure, but it seems safe to say that they all somehow stem from people trying to make sense of the world around them. There are certainly religious or societal undertones to some. It's interesting to hypothesize on these, but we can at least say that although vampires were believed to pass on vampirism, there were various other causes, some of which were quite enigmatic.

-《《◆》》-

Endnotes

1. Barber, *Vampires, Burial and Death*, 16–18.
2. Ibid.
3. Ibid.
4. Ibid., 16–19.
5. *Acten-mäßige und Umständliche Relation von denen Vampiren oder Menschen-Saugern* (Leipzig: Augusto Martini, 1732), 11. https://books.google.com/books?id=etRZAAAAcAAJ.
6. Barber, *Vampires, Burial and Death*, 6–7.
7. D'Argens, *The Jewish Spy*, 123.
8. Murgoci, "The Vampire in Roumania," 56–57.
9. Vukanović, "The Vampire," 237.
10. Ralston, *The Songs of the Russian People*, 412.
11. Bowman, *The Crimes of the Oedipodean Cycle*, 47.
12. Summers, *Vampires and Vampirism*, 140.
13. Vukanović, "The Vampire," 238–239.

8

unlight

aving already covered staking and decapitation, it seems like we're at a good point to turn our sights toward the sun—another standard way of dispatching the undead. On screen, vampires are often destroyed by sunlight, with those bright rays burning their skin and reducing them to ashes, or perhaps a skeleton. They're certainly not morning people, and I get that. At face value, this vulnerability of theirs certainly makes sense. Why wouldn't sunlight purge away these evil, nocturnal creatures? Well, I'm afraid we have another major disconnect between fiction and folklore here. Traditionally, sunlight does NOT kill vampires. It would seem that no villager ever believed that sunshine would permanently rid the populace of these blood-sucking menaces.

So, does sunlight do anything at all? Well, it depends on the place. In most of the stories we've discussed thus far, such as the cases of Plogojowitz and Paole, the vampires have been nocturnal, attacking people in their sleep. Nothing is specifically mentioned in regard to daylight, one way or the other. However, given that staking and burning are much more involved tasks than just exposing a vampire to sunlight, one can presume that this simpler option didn't factor into the people's beliefs.

Not all accounts omit details regarding daylight. In the story of the shoemaker of Breslau (which I discussed in chapter 5), it states, "there appears a Spectrum in the exact shape and habit of the deceased, and that not only in the night but at Midday."[1] The story makes it clear that this undead visitor was able to move about during the day. It's important to note, though, that the story goes into detail about how the shoemaker tormented people at night. Aside from this line about being seen at midday, the vampire's daytime activities aren't further discussed—but the sunlight certainly didn't stop him.

The Greek *vrykolakas* was also believed to be able to walk around in the daylight. Those working in the fields or traveling along the roads could potentially encounter one of these undead creatures. Its fearsome appearance alone was enough to kill, though it was sometimes thought to strangle its victims. Of course, the *vrykolakas* wasn't believed to prefer sunshine or anything like that. Nighttime was when it was usually active, but it wasn't confined to the sunless hours.[2]

So, does the sun ever do anything to vampires? By shifting from Greece to Russia, we get somewhat closer to our modern expectations. In one folktale, a solider passing a graveyard at night suddenly realized that a corpse was chasing after him. The soldier temporarily evaded his undead pursuer and headed for a little chapel he had spotted nearby. Upon entering, he found another corpse, this one lying on a table with candles burning. Quite frightened by what was happening, the soldier concealed himself in a corner of the building. Shortly afterward, the original corpse burst into the chapel, looking for its prey. The body on the table then suddenly got up and the two corpses began arguing about who would get to eat the soldier. The exchange of words then turned to brawling. The fighting lasted so long that the roosters begin to crow (undoubtedly signaling daylight), and both bodies collapsed to the ground. With the undead now inanimate, the solder was able to continue on his way. Interestingly, as the soldier was thanking God for his escape, he referred to the corpses as "wizards."[3] This is likely from the belief that practitioners of dark magic become vampires after death.

It's important to note that although this story ends with the corpses becoming lifeless at daybreak, it's doubtful this condition was permanent. Rather, it's likely the corpses would awaken again that night. To support this, we need only look at another Russian folktale with some similar elements. In this story, a solider encountered an undead warlock one night and learned some of his secrets. The warlock ended up trying to kill the solider, but then turned back into a lifeless corpse when the rooster crowed. The story makes it clear, though, that this effect is only temporary. To truly rid themselves of the warlock, the soldier and the local peasants gathered aspen wood for a fire, burned the corpse, and killed any creatures (such as birds, insects, and reptiles) that emerged from it. The ashes were then thrown to the winds and peace was restored.[4]

In regard to daybreak, both stories mention the corpses becoming lifeless when a rooster crows. I think most people hearing these tales would assume the bird's crowing is a storytelling device—the rooster signifying that the sun is rising, and it is the dawning of the day that immobilizes the vampires. However, there's another tale that calls this assumption into question. In it, a sacristan must read psalms over the corpse of man who led a very sinful life. During these readings, at the hour of midnight, the dead man sprang to life. With mouth wide open, the corpse lunged toward the sacristan. Luckily, this officer of the church had come prepared. He had brought a rooster with him, and, as the dead man approached, he pinched the bird. This caused the rooster to crow, and the corpse immediately became lifeless once more![5] In this story, it is clear that the crowing, in and of itself, returned the undead man to a lifeless state. One wonders if the rooster's crow has some intrinsic power, or perhaps the vampire was simply fooled into thinking it was morning.

It would seem that, at best, sunlight might temporarily revert folkloric vampires to an inanimate state. At worst, sunlight does nothing at all.

If this is the case, where did our modern notions regarding this vampiric vulnerability come from? So far, we've found that a number of traits are a product of nineteenth-century fiction—but not this one. None of those early fictional vampires were destroyed by the sun. Even in the immensely influential *Dracula*, the eponymous count moves about in the daytime. His abilities are limited because of it, but it's certainly not fatal to him.

To find the original source for this now-accepted piece of vampire lore, we actually have to look to the silver screen.

In 1922, the German film *Nosferatu, eine Symphonie des Grauens* (in English, *Nosferatu, a Symphony of Horror*) was released. As you may have guessed from the date, it was a black-and-white silent movie. *Nosferatu* was based on the *Dracula* novel, but the production company, Prana Film, never acquired the rights. As such, a number of story details were changed to avoid copyright infringement. Unfortunately for the studio, its attempt was in vain, and Florence Stoker, Bram's widow, sued the company. Prana Film lost the case, and the court ruled that all copies of the film were to be destroyed. Luckily for us, some prints survived this purge, and we still have the movie today.

As I mentioned, various details were changed in *Nosferatu* to differ it from *Dracula*. Besides the obvious new title, character names were altered, including that of the main antagonist. In *Nosferatu*, the vampire is known as Count Orlok, played by Max Schreck, and his appearance is quite striking. Bald, with pointed ears, long fingernails, and ratlike front fangs, Orlok is truly memorable, and you've likely seen images of him, or based on him, in popular media.

For the purposes of this chapter, a major difference in *Nosferatu* that we need to discuss is how the vampire is ultimately destroyed. In *Dracula*, the count is pursued by the heroes of the novel and stabbed with a knife (that's right, not even a wooden stake) through the heart. Things go quite differently for Count Orlok. In the film, the character Ellen reads about a method to destroy vampires. It requires that a maiden willingly sacrifice her blood, essentially occupying the vampire so he will be unaware that dawn is approaching. Orlok does indeed come for Ellen in the night and feeds on her until morning. As the count is exiting her room, he passes a window just as the sun rises over the horizon. The evil count dramatically turns in reaction to the sunlight and then vanishes. In his place, smoke rises from the floor. It is this classic scene that gives us the first occurrence of a vampire being killed by the rays of the sun.

Interestingly, Dr. Raymond T. McNally, who was a professor and vampire scholar, suggested that there could be a somewhat different explanation of the film's finale. It's possible that the sunlight alone didn't kill Count Orlok. Rather, it may have been the culmination of the entire ritual, which also included the sacrifice of a willing victim.[6] If that is indeed the case, the subsequent works of fiction that were inspired by *Nosferatu* may have been based on a slight misinterpretation of the scene.

Regardless of the particulars, it seems that sunlight has only been lethal to vampires since the early 1920s, and, when you think about it, this actually isn't that surprising. In the documented accounts, such as the cases of Plogojowitz and Paole, the villagers were motivated by what must have been a profound fear. It seems unlikely that simply leaving a vampiric corpse out in the sun for a little while would have satisfied them. Such an approach just wouldn't have provided the catharsis that they were craving. It was only with the vampire's evolution in fiction, where sunlight could have an immediate and dramatic effect, that this became part of our modern conventions. Next time you're watching a movie where a vampire turns to dust as the sun rises, you can thank a black-and-white, expressionist film for setting the trend.

⁓«‹•›»⁓

Endnotes

1. More, *An Antidote against Atheism*, 210.
2. Summers, *Vampires and Vampirism*, 30–31.
3. Ralston, *Russian Folk-Tales*, 316–317.
4. Ibid., 320–321.
5. Ralston, *The Songs of the Russian People*, 415.
6. Raymond T. McNally, *Dracula: Truth and Terror* (Irvington, NY: Voyager, 1996), CD-ROM, audio commentary for *Nosferatu*.

9

Garlic

arlic is another old standby in the vampire hunter's arsenal. It often appears in fiction, where it serves as a vampire repellent. Pop culture imagery seems to favor cloves of the pungent plant arranged in a string, perhaps for easy hanging. Interestingly, in the *Dracula* novel, Dr. Van Helsing uses the plant's flower, rather than the bulb, to keep the count at bay. The book also has garlic playing a role in the actual slaying of a vampire. After the vampiric Lucy Westenra is staked and decapitated (as we discussed in chapter 5), Dr. Van Helsing and Dr. Seward take the extra precaution of stuffing her mouth with garlic. The plant has become a staple of our modern-day vampire mythos, and I don't doubt that *Dracula* and its myriad adaptations had a hand in that.

But, as we always do, we must turn to the folklore. Was this garlic weakness simply an invention of Bram Stoker, or was there a time when people truly believed in this plant's protective powers? Well, if you thought that garlic seemed too peculiar a detail to be plucked out of thin air, you'd be right. It does indeed feature in folklore.

In 1885, an article was published entitled *Transylvanian Superstitions*, written by Emily Gerard. In it, Gerard discusses the various beliefs she encountered while living in Transylvania, including those concerning vampires. In regard to garlic, Gerard discusses how, for "obstinate cases" of vampirism, the head may be removed and the mouth stuffed with garlic.[1] It's no coincidence that this is exactly what the good doctors Van Helsing and Seward did to the undead Lucy. We know from Stoker's notes that he referenced Gerard's article while writing his novel.[2]

Of course, Gerard isn't the only author to discuss the use of garlic in vampire traditions. Agnes Murgoci's 1926 essay, *The Vampire in Roumania* (which I've cited previously in this book), provides some excellent details. For example, this work also mentions the custom of placing garlic into the mouth of the corpse—a practice that might be done when there was suspicion that the deceased may become a vampire. Interestingly, there was also a belief that those who didn't eat garlic were, in fact, vampires.[3]

Murgoci's essay goes on to discuss how garlic was used to protect the home. At certain times of the year when vampires were especially likely to be about, garlic would be placed on the door to the house and on everything inside. Windows would be anointed with it in the shape of the Christian cross, and it would be rubbed into keyholes and the chimney (as these were considered to be other points of entry for a vampire). Even the cattle would get this garlic treatment.[4]

When you consider the beliefs surrounding garlic identified by Murgoci as well as Gerard, it seems that this plant could potentially play a role in all phases of vampire hunting: detection, deterrence, and destruction. It's a handy resource indeed, and one that has certainly endured in fiction.

You may be wondering why garlic had such an effect on vampires. What was it about this plant in particular that made it an effective defense? The first thing to consider is that garlic had a special reputation even in ancient times. In the Roman Empire, it was believed to have a wide variety of medicinal uses, including healing wounds, relieving toothaches, and curing coughs, to name a few. Surprisingly, it was also thought to be an aphrodisiac. Less surprisingly, its smell was believed to repel snakes and scorpions. Garlic even had religious significance to the ancient Egyptians.[5] Perhaps these traditions evolved over time, such that the plant eventually came to be associated with protection against vampires.

If garlic's effect on the undead was the result of a natural progression, why exactly did vampires get singled out for this weakness? Remarkably, they're not the only creatures in folklore to have this vulnerability. For example, in Romanian traditions, garlic was also thought to be able to keep wolves and evil spirits away.[6] In Greece, garlic was used to ward off the effects of the evil eye.[7] Garlic's usefulness, at least in terms of folkloric beliefs, just seems to grow the further one digs.

There's an interesting explanation concerning garlic and vampires that I'd like to discuss—and it relates to aroma. As one might expect, vampires were often believed to have a very foul smell. Garlic, as we all know, is also particularly strong smelling. Essentially, the idea is that the garlic odor would overpower the stench of the vampire, and this, in some way, would repel the vampire itself.[8] It would seem that a practical use of garlic was extended to a supernatural use.

Anyway you slice it (or chop it, or press it), garlic is certainly an interesting plant when it comes to folklore. Beliefs regarding it are ancient, and it seems inextricably tied to uses far beyond that of adding flavor. I have only scratched the surface here in regard to this enigmatic plant, but it certainly seems clear that popular fiction has ensured that garlic's place in vampire lore will endure.

-‹‹‹◆›››-

Endnotes

1. Emily Gerard, "Transylvanian Superstitions," *Nineteenth Century* 18 (London, 1885), 130–50; reprinted in Emily Gerard and Agnes Murgoci, *Transylvanian Superstitions* (Scripta Minora, 2013), 29.
2. Bram Stoker, *Bram Stoker's Notes for Dracula: A Facsimile Edition*, eds. Robert Eighteen-Bisang and Elizabeth Miller (Jefferson, NC: McFarland, 2008), 121.
3. Murgoci, "The Vampire in Roumania," 55–56, 62.
4. Ibid., 55, 62.
5. Pliny (the Elder), *The Natural History of Pliny*, vol. 4, trans. John Bostock and H. T. Riley (London: Henry G. Bohn, 1856), 171, 225–228. https://books.google.com/books?id=IUoMAAAAIAAJ.
6. Murgoci, "The Vampire in Roumania," 62.
7. F. C. Pouqueville, *Travels in the Morea, Albania, and Other Parts of the Ottoman Empire*, trans. Anne Plumptre (London: Henry Colburn, 1813), 129–130. https://books.google.com/books?id=Ar9BAAAAYAAJ.
8. Barber, *Vampires, Burial and Death*, 131–132; McNally, "Interview with the Vampire Expert," in *Dracula: Truth and Terror*.

10

irrors

In Universal's classic 1931 horror film *Dracula*, the sinister count's true nature is revealed through, of all things, a cigarette box. How could such a modest object prove to be so important? Quite simple—it had a mirror inside the lid. After Jonathan Harker opens the box to retrieve a cigarette, the astute Dr. Van Helsing notices that Dracula casts no reflection in it. To investigate further, Van Helsing approaches the count and shows him the box. Dracula angrily knocks it out of Van Helsing's hands and abruptly, but courteously, takes his leave. It's a great scene, with actor Bela Lugosi communicating a lot through the intensity of his gaze. It's also a fine example of how, in the movies, vampires don't usually have reflections.

Of course, as we've learned, traditional beliefs don't always match up to our modern expectations—and this appears to be another one of those cases. The old tales and accounts don't appear to mention anything about vampires lacking reflections. Given that the established signs of vampirism were often discussed in these stories, you would presume that people would have mentioned mirrors if they were relevant. It seems safe to assume that the vampires of folklore could see themselves in the looking glass and would probably notice some bloodstains while doing so.

With that said, mirrors aren't entirely unconnected from vampire mythology. There was a Romani belief that a corpse would turn into a vampire if it saw itself in a mirror. To avoid this situation, all the mirrors in a house would be covered while a dead body was there.[1] Interestingly, the tradition of covering mirrors after a recent passing has been found in various European countries and beyond. However, the common explanation for the practice doesn't concern vampires. Rather, the belief was that a person might die if they saw their reflection shortly after a death had occurred. This could happen because the ghost of the deceased might take the person's soul, since it was being reflected in the glass. In Burma, it seems the opposite was true. A mirror might be placed next to a corpse to prevent a living person's soul from following after the deceased.[2]

It would seem that mirrors, regardless of the particulars, were often believed to have some kind of relevance when it came to death and the spirit.

Now that we have a better sense of where mirrors do fit into folklore, let's discuss when vampires originally lost their reflections. The first work of fiction to include this detail would appear to be the novel *Dracula*. It looks like we have the imagination of Bram Stoker to thank for our unreflective undead. The notes he made while writing *Dracula* also mention the count's inability to be photographed, cast a shadow, or even be painted.[3] Essentially, it seems that a visual record of the vampire simply could not come into existence. When trying to answer the question of why Stoker added this, a common explanation draws on the mirror's folkloric connections to the soul. Essentially, through the count's lack of reflection, Stoker may have been implying that Dracula was soulless. It is a fascinating example of how, through fiction, folk beliefs can be adapted and expanded upon.

-«‹◆›»-

Endnotes

1. Vukanović, "The Vampire," 236.
2. J. G. Frazer, *The Golden Bough: A Study in Magic and Religion*, vol. 3, 3rd ed. (London: Macmillan, 1914), 51–52, 94–95. https://books.google.com/books?id=f9w3AQAAMAAJ.
3. Stoker, *Bram Stoker's Notes for Dracula*, 19, 21.

11

Religious
Objects

orks of fiction often include the vampire having some kind of fear or aversion to religious objects, normally Christian in nature. Think of the hero holding up a wooden cross to repel the advancing undead. Holy water and even a Communion wafer may also feature in the story as powerful aids. Sometimes this trait is deliberately omitted, especially in modern tales, in which vampirism can have a scientific explanation (such as a virus). However, if we are dealing with the supernatural sort, these sacred items can be invaluable. When describing Dracula's weaknesses, Van Helsing tells us, "as for things sacred, as this symbol, my crucifix . . . to them he is nothing, but in their presence he take his place far off and silent with respect."[1]

I don't think it will come as a surprise to anyone that this vulnerability can be found in folklore. It certainly stands to reason, and religious beliefs and rituals have already come up in some of this book's previous chapters. However, this theme is not omnipresent. For example, in the well-documented cases of Peter Plogojowitz and Arnod Paole, the record remains silent on the use of religious objects. Thankfully, I was able to dig up some other accounts.

First, let's start with an example of how a cross is used. Back in chapter 6, I mentioned a Russian tale where a vampire entered a house and filled a pail with the blood of the occupants. What I didn't mention was how he was able to gain access. That story actually begins with a peasant driving his wagon past a cemetery, where he agreed to give a stranger a ride. When they got to the village, they found that the gates to various houses were wide open. However, the stranger referred to them all as being "Shut tight!" It turns out that those gates had crosses branded into them. At the last house, the gates were closed and secured with an immense lock—but no cross. Those gates magically opened to the stranger, who entered the house and drained the occupants of their blood. After finishing, the vampire noticed that dawn was approaching, and he instantly transported both himself and the peasant driver back to the graveyard. The peasant would have then likely been the vampire's next victim, but the rooster began to crow and the undead stranger disappeared.[2] The story makes the obvious point that the crosses alone were able to keep the vampire at bay. It was the spiritual barrier, not the physical one, that proved effective. We may also take this story as a warning against picking up hitchhikers, especially by graveyards!

Let's now look to holy water. We see its use in the *vrykolakas* panic observed by Tournefort in 1700. The populace had priests sprinkling holy water around the houses and even washing doors with it. Additionally, holy water was poured into the mouth of the *vrykolakas* itself. Unfortunately, these tactics proved entirely ineffective as far as the villagers were concerned.[3] For another example, we can look to one Romanian practice discussed by Agnes Murgoci. She explains that a vampire would be exhumed and undressed. The clothes would be put back into the coffin, sprinkled with holy water, and then reburied. The body would be put in a sack, taken to the forest, and then cut up and burned in the manner discussed back in chapter 4.[4] In this case, the holy water seems to be an element of the vampire destruction ritual, rather than an apotropaic (a means of warding off evil).

I'd like to take this opportunity to expand upon the use of water as a tool against vampires. While holy water would be effective due to its religious significance, nature's rivers, streams, and even seas could also be of use. For example, there was a belief in Romania that suicide victims should be placed in running water in order to prevent them from turning into vampires. It was also thought that vampires would float in water.[5] According to a Greek tale, vampires are unable to cross salt water and were thus safely banished to an uninhabited island.[6] Additionally, some Romani traditions held that vampires couldn't pass over water.[7] I'll also mention that in some parts of Transylvania, there was a practice of funeral processions walking through a river or stream on their return home. This would prevent the soul of the deceased from following them.[8] In these cases, we see evidence of the connection between the natural world and the supernatural one. This detail even finds its way into Stoker's novel, with Van Helsing saying, "It is said, too, that he [Dracula] can only pass running water at the slack or the flood of the tide."[9]

Let's turn our sights back toward the topic at hand—religious objects. I'd like to end by briefly discussing Communion wafers. Although Dr. Van Helsing uses them in the *Dracula* novel, they don't seem to be mentioned often in vampire folklore. There are a couple of tales where the sacred wafers are used to keep the dead from rising, but in those cases the deceased weren't actually harming anyone. For example, one tale involves a young, sixth-century priest who died unexpectedly. Unfortunately for him, he died in a state of sin, since he had left his monastery without the permission of the abbot, St. Benedict. After being buried in consecrated ground, the earth rejected the priest, and his body was found aboveground the next day. His family then contacted St. Benedict for help, and he gave them a Communion wafer to put on the dead priest's chest. After the priest was reburied with this wafer, he remained in his grave.[10]

Given the malevolent supernatural qualities of the folkloric vampire, it's certainly not surprising that villagers would turn to that which is blessed and sacred as a means of protection. Quite simply, it's good overpowering evil. This vulnerability to sacred objects has certainly survived into the popular culture of today. However, as more sci-fi-based vampires emerge in modern fiction, one wonders if this particular characteristic may fade over time.

-‹‹‹•›››-

Endnotes

1. Stoker, *Dracula*, 245–246.
2. Ralston, *The Songs of the Russian People*, 411–412.
3. Tournefort, *A Voyage into the Levant*, 146.
4. Murgoci, "The Vampire in Roumania," 52–53.
5. Ibid., 55, 60.
6. Rennell Rodd, *The Customers and Lore of Modern Greece*, 2nd ed. (London: David Stott, 1892), 194. https://books.google.com/books?id=k-fYAAAAMAAJ.
7. Vukanović, "The Vampire," 237.
8. Emily Gerard, *The Land beyond the Forest*, vol. 1, *Facts, Figures, and Fancies from Transylvania* (Edinburgh: William Blackwood and Sons, 1888), 316. https://books.google.com/books?id=nDY_AAAAYAAJ.
9. Stoker, *Dracula*, 245.
10. Calmet, *The Phantom World*, 290.

12

Coffins and Graves

Fictional vampires usually prefer sleeping accommodations that are in keeping with their undead nature. Simply put, they go for a coffin rather than a bed. The location of this coffin could be in a crypt, dungeon, or somewhere else appropriately atmospheric. This can certainly be the case in folklore as well. For example, in one tale set in Poland, a burial vault is found to be in a state of disarray, and it's assumed that the corpse of the most recent arrival is to blame.[1] I've already mentioned a number of suspected vampires that were exhumed from their graves. Depending on the time and place, those burials may or may not have involved a coffin. Ultimately, though, the notion of a vampire resting in a place associated with interment is certainly not an invention of fiction.

With that said, it seems like this is shaping up to be a short chapter. However, there's an aspect to this topic that I'd like to explore. Specifically, how did the vampires of folklore leave and return to their graves? In fiction, the vampire's coffin is often not buried in the ground. The undead can simply push open the lid (preferably slowly and dramatically) and climb out. What if there was six feet of earth on top of it?

There are a few different angles to explore here, but let's begin with a British tale dating back to at least 1197. The story involves a priest who served as chaplain to a wealthy woman. He spent a great deal of his time focused on earthly, rather than spiritual, pursuits. In particular, he had such an affinity for hunting that he was nicknamed *Hundeprest* (translating to "dog priest"). After his death, he was buried at the monastery of Melrose in Scotland. Apparently, the disregard he had shown for his religious order caused him to rise from his grave at night. The monks were able to prevent him from entering the monastery, but nothing was stopping him from visiting his former patroness. He would routinely enter her bedchamber and terrify her with his groaning and murmuring—though the story never mentions any physical harm coming to her. This woman pleads for help, and the monks decide to assist her.[2]

Two friars and two young men go to the graveyard at night to wait for the *Hundeprest*. After staying out until after midnight, three members of the team decide to go to a nearby house to get warm, while one of the monks chooses to stay behind. It is at this point that the *Hundeprest*, sensing that it was an opportune moment, rises from his grave and starts rushing toward the remaining friar. As the undead priest approaches, the friar strikes him with an axe, making a deep wound. The *Hundeprest* then starts retreating toward his tomb, with the friar running after him. When the undead priest arrives back, the text states that the grave, "which opening of its own accord, and receiving its guest from the advance of the pursuer, immediately appeared to close again with the same facility." At this point, the friar's three compatriots arrive. At dawn, the team digs up the corpse and sees the axe wound that had been inflicted. They then carry the corpse outside the monastery walls, burn it, and scatter the ashes.[3]

In this story, the ground supernaturally opens and closes, allowing the vampire to exit and reenter his tomb as needed. It's certainly not subtle, but it allows for a vampire that is entirely and consistently physical in nature. Plus, this detail adds a bold and exciting element to the tale. Although this seems like an effective explanation of how vampires get out and about, it's not the only one.

To further explore this idea, let's now shift to Romania. In that country, there was a belief that you could identify the grave of a vampire by the presence of a hole in the ground near the tombstone. Although this hole only had to be large enough for a snake to pass through, villagers believed it was the means by which the vampire would leave its grave.[4] Outside Romania, certain Romani groups also shared this kind of belief. Additionally, they held that pouring boiling water into such an opening would kill a newly created vampire.[5] With this explanation, the vampire's corporeal nature is somewhat compromised. Because it must be able to shrink or alter its body in some way to escape, it is more than purely a revived corpse. It now possesses some additional supernatural qualities.

To get a different take on how vampires escape their graves, we can turn to eighteenth-century church scholar Dom Calmet. He discussed the idea that if vampires were real, one explanation for their existence might be that the devil was animating the bodies of the dead. Calmet then further wondered if the devil could give the corpses physical properties similar to air and water, such that these vampires could evaporate through the ground without needing to shift it. It's important to note, though, that Calmet then goes on to question the likelihood of such a scenario.[6] This notion of the vampire taking on a mist-like form actually fits quite nicely with the events in Stoker's *Dracula*.

Dom Calmet also mentioned a belief held by some people that vampires were actually illusions, not physical corpses rising from the ground. He acknowledged that humans were incapable of producing such manifestations, but raised the question if angels or demons could.[7] This explanation is an interesting one, and it would certainly explain why the graves of supposed vampires would be undisturbed. It also fundamentally shifts the nature of a vampire to being entirely incorporeal.

Before finishing our discussion, let's look at one more explanation that serves as a unique compromise. Some Romani believed that the deceased's body would not leave the grave at all. Instead, only their ghost would exit the tomb. At this point, their spirit would receive a new body with which to move around in. This vampiric physical form would have extremely long hair and, when moving, would have a mist-like effect surrounding it.[8] It's unclear where this new body comes from, but this concept provides an interesting blend of corporeal and incorporeal qualities.

Ultimately, as we are dealing with supernatural beliefs, there is no final consensus on how exactly a vampire exits its grave. In many cases, such as the one involving Peter Plogojowitz, the topic isn't even addressed. Perhaps the otherworldly nature of the whole affair meant that such a detail didn't need explaining. Or perhaps people were so frightened that it didn't really matter. Regardless, it would seem that folkloric vampires somehow got out of their graves, and that's that.

-<<<•>>>-

Endnotes

1. Calmet, *The Phantom World*, 278.
2. Newburgh, *The History of William Newburgh*, 658–659.
3. Ibid., 659.
4. Murgoci, "The Vampire in Roumania," 54.
5. Vukanović, "The Vampire," 243, 249.
6. Calmet, *The Phantom World*, 358–359.
7. Ibid., 360.
8. Vukanović, "The Vampire," 239.

13

ilver Bullets

In this book's introduction, I discussed silver bullets as being part of the famed and controversial vampire killing kits. Now that we've covered many of the well-established vampire traits and built up a solid picture of the folkloric vampire, it seems time to return to this metallic topic. I will first say that silver bullets or related items are not unheard of in popular culture. A well-known example would be the 1998 film *Blade*, which has vampires that are vulnerable to silver weapons. The TV series *True Blood* (2008–2014) also includes a silver weakness. Another big-screen example would be *The Satanic Rites of Dracula* (1973) from Hammer Film Productions, in which a silver bullet is presented as a potential weapon against the count. Going back to Stoker's novel, we don't find silver bullets per se. However, when describing the count's weaknesses, Van Helsing states, "a sacred bullet fired into the coffin kill him so that he be true dead."[1] We're left to wonder what constitutes a sacred bullet, but it certainly seems to be in the same vein.

Before we dive headfirst into beliefs surrounding silver, I'd first like to focus on bullets alone. Normally we would assume that a lead bullet would be entirely useless against a vampire. However, while doing research, I ran across something rather surprising. It's exemplified in an account from 1873 in which the area around Stryi, Ukraine, was being afflicted with cholera. The farmers believed that an evil spirit (*bösen Geist*) was the cause of the illness, with suspicion falling upon Mikolaj Macewko, the deceased mayor from Tuchla. For guidance, the people turned to Olega Ilkon, the mayor from Libossura. He had Macewko's corpse exhumed and stakes were driven into its head, right rib, and back. Additionally (and this is the part that's rather intriguing), Ilkon fired a bullet into the dead man's body. Finally, the corpse was cut apart, and the farmers took pieces of it to ward off the cholera epidemic.[2]

In this case, it would appear that shooting the corpse with a regular (nonsilver) bullet was part of the vampire destruction ritual. This practice may certainly seem surprising to modern vampire fans, but it's actually not an isolated occurrence in history. Emily Gerard noted in her article about Transylvanian beliefs that there existed a custom of firing a bullet into the vampire's coffin as an alternative to using a stake.[3] Given that we know Bram Stoker had seen this article, it seems quite likely that it influenced Van Helsing's line in the novel.

Another example of regular bullets can be found in the vampire traditions of the Romani. There was one practice where those wishing to slay a vampire would leave a hen's egg in a location where the creature was likely to appear. They would then conceal themselves and wait. If the egg disappeared, this would be taken as an indication that the vampire was present. (It's important to note that vampires were believed to be invisible to most people, so that's why this egg trap was necessary.) Once this happened, the concealed hunters would fire at the general area, hoping to kill the monster.[4]

So, we've established that there's a rather surprising precedent for regular bullets harming vampires, but let's get back to the true topic at hand. What about silver bullets? Did this metal have some special effect? Well, Montague Summers, in his 1929 book, rather definitively states that there was a belief in some Slavic countries that a vampire could be killed by a blessed silver bullet.[5]

Based on that, it certainly seems like an open-and-shut case. However, Summers gives no additional details on this. He doesn't specify the countries or mention where he found this information. It's a tantalizing detail, but something of a dead end. Thankfully, though, our hunt doesn't stop there.

One rather intriguing reference I found was actually from a question printed in a UK publication in 1890. The writer had seen an advertisement in a French newspaper that told a story about a vampire that inhabited Snowdon (the tallest mountain in Wales). This monster would kill any young person who ventured too close to its lair. It would consume its victim's blood and thus extend its life by however many years that person would have lived. The vampire was eventually destroyed by a silver bullet to the head. The writer had wanted to know if any of the readers had heard of this tale before.[6] Finding this reference was pretty exciting, but given that the source was apparently an advertisement, it's hard to say if this tale represents an actual folkloric belief. Still, it certainly illustrates that the notion of using silver bullets against vampires existed in the late nineteenth century.

The best evidence for silver bullets in folklore seems to be found in Paul Barber's book on the scientific explanations of vampire legends (which I've referenced previously). In it, he mentions a Serbian immigrant who discussed the practice of taking a silver coin with a cross on it and breaking that coin into four pieces. Those fragments would then be loaded into a shotgun shell and fired at a vampire in order to kill it. Later in the book, an account from an East German immigrant is mentioned, which includes storing silver knives under mattresses and cribs. Their presence would ward off vampires and werewolves.[7] These two accounts serve as clear examples that there have been actual beliefs regarding the effectiveness of silver against the undead.

Aside from Barber's finds and the mysterious Snowdon vampire, most other references to silver in vampire lore seem to be a stretch at best. For example, in a nineteenth-century account of the beliefs in Turkey, it's mentioned that amulets are used to keep the *vrykolakas* and other evil creatures at bay. These amulets could consist of silver crosses, or other religious imagery, containing small pieces of what was believed to be the true cross.[8] Although silver is mentioned, it's unclear as to how essential the material was. It could be that the actual power of the amulet came solely from the true cross and religious imagery, with the silver being purely decorative. As I said, it's a bit of a stretch.

I'd also like to briefly discuss a tale from eastern Serbia that involves a creature known as an *ala*. In the story, one appears as a man while another has the form of an eagle. At one point, the human-shaped *ala* is described as being someone's father, so it may be that the creature was once a normal person. It eats vast quantities of food and has the ability to create hailstorms, thus destroying crops. In order to kill this threat, the *ala* must be fired at with a shotgun containing four pellets, each of a different metal: lead, silver, gold, and steel. A peasant ends up using this approach to save his harvest from devastation.[9] The story certainly contains the element of a silver bullet, but it's only part of the overall equation. It's also arguable as to whether we can really categorize an *ala* as a vampire. Ultimately, just like with the silver amulet, this example may be a reach.

As you've probably noticed in this book, sometimes the lines between ghosts and vampires can get a little blurry. Therefore, it may not be surprising that silver also figures in some ghost lore. In the nineteenth century, a belief was documented in the US state of Georgia that a silver bullet would kill a ghost. Additionally, it was thought that constructing the deceased's coffin with silver nails and screws could prevent hauntings.[10] Given the corporeal aspect of vampires, this last detail ties in nicely. Clearly, with this belief, there was some physical link between the ghost and the corpse. It seems likely the idea was that the ghost was unable to leave the grave when it was surrounded by silver.

When talking about silver bullets, one type of monster usually comes to mind—and it's not vampires or ghosts. Naturally, I'm referring to werewolves. The use of silver against these beasts has really been cemented in pop culture. Given this, I feel as if I would be remiss if I didn't go into a little of the actual lore. It was already mentioned that werewolves could be repelled by silver knives—but what about bullets? Well, I was pleased to learn that the folklore supports what Hollywood has taught us. There were indeed beliefs that werewolves were impervious to traditional weapons but could be harmed if shot with silver ammunition. Additionally, it was thought that iron and steel could revert these monsters back into their human forms. To keep a werewolf at bay, a sword could be placed in the ground with its point directed toward the creature.[11] It's interesting how metal of various types could affect this creature. Just like with vampires, there's more to werewolf lore than we might realize. We'll dive deeper into this in a later chapter.

Silver's usefulness doesn't stop here, though. There are various tales of silver bullets being used against the malevolent witches that inhabit folklore. For example, in a legend from Perthshire, Scotland, we find an English doctor spending the night in a mountain cottage while on a hunting trip. At a very late hour, as the doctor was sitting with his hunting dogs around him, a cat entered the room. Strangely, the dogs did not react, and the cat proceeded to sit with its back toward the fire. This feline then began to grow until it was roughly the size of a young cow. To deal with this threat, the doctor removed a silver button from his clothing and loaded it into his gun. He fired at the creature and it quickly ran out of the cottage. The next day, as the doctor was heading toward the valley, he was asked to visit a farmer's wife who had become ill. While treating her, he ended up removing an object that was lodged in her right breast—it was his silver button.[12]

You may be wondering why silver is so useful against monsters. Unfortunately, most sources never really delve into this. It's often just stated as a matter of fact. However, if we look at ancient beliefs regarding this metal, a possible explanation does arise. There's an interesting interplay among silver, the moon, and the classical goddess Diana. Due to its color, silver has been associated with the moon since ancient times. It was a connection reflected in astrology and alchemy.[13] In Roman mythology, Diana was the goddess of the moon and was connected with that metal. Diana was also known as being a protector of women (especially during childbirth), children, and cattle. Interestingly, silver amulets bearing Diana-related symbols were worn as protection against the evil eye even in the modern era. There are also examples of ancient silver amulets containing symbols related to various gods (including Diana) that were used for warding off the evil eye.[14] Perhaps silver's mystical association with protection was extended over time, turning it into a material suitable for a weapon to fight supernatural creatures.

As we've learned, silver bullets aren't limited to dealing with a single type of evil creature. For the record, even sea monsters were believed to be vulnerable to these pricey projectiles![15] Although silver doesn't have a substantial presence in vampire lore, it's not entirely absent. When specifically considering the undead, perhaps their silver weakness is due to a diffusion of beliefs from tales concerning witches and werewolves. It may have seemed like a logical extension that a weapon useful against one type of supernatural entity would also work against others. I'll also note that in regard to witches and werewolves, silver seems to be used when the culprit is in a nonhuman state, such as a cat or a wolf. While they are in an animal form, we are left to believe that ordinary weapons would be ineffective. Perhaps we can apply the same line of thinking to vampires. Could it be that since the vampiric state itself is unnatural, it is thus susceptible to silver? Of course, given that some beliefs allowed for vampires to be killed by standard bullets, it's not surprising that silver has never had a strong foothold. Still, it adds a level of flair that, I think, works well these days.

Endnotes

1. Stoker, *Dracula*, 246.
2. "Grabesschändung hilft gegen Cholera."
3. Gerard, "Transylvanian Superstitions," 29.
4. Vukanović, "The Vampire," 248.
5. Summers, *Vampires and Vampirism*, 209.
6. France, "The Vampire of Snowdon," in *Bye-gones: Relating to Wales and the Border Counties, 1889–1890*, 2nd ser., vol. 1, ed. John Askew Roberts (Oswestry, UK: Woodall, Minshall, 1890), 307. https://books.google.com/books?id=ht4GAAAAYAAJ.
7. Barber, *Vampires, Burial and Death*, 54, 63.
8. Blunt, *The People of Turkey*, 224–225.
9. Jan Louis Perkowski, *Vampire Lore: From the Writings of Jan Louis Perkowski* (Bloomington, IN: Slavica, 2006), 358–360.
10. Tom Peete Cross, "Witchcraft in North Carolina," in *Studies in Philology*, vol. 16, eds. Edwin Greenlaw, William M. Dey, and George Howe (Chapel Hill: University of North Carolina, 1919), 285. https://books.google.com/books?id=m65JAAAAYAAJ.
11. Walter K. Kelly, *Curiosities of Indo-European Tradition and Folk-Lore* (London: Chapman & Hall, 1863), 259. https://books.google.com/books?id=2XXYAAAAMAAJ; Conway, *Demonology and Devil-Lore*, 314.
12. John Gregorson Campbell, *Witchcraft & Second Sight in the Highlands and Islands of Scotland: Tales and Traditions Collected Entirely from Oral Sources* (Glasgow: James MacLehose and Sons, 1902) 49–50. https://books.google.com/books?id=shnXAAAAMAAJ.
13. Timothy Harley, *Moon Lore* (London: Swan Sonnenschein, Le Bas, & Lowrey, 1885), 219. https://books.google.com/books?id=ShwHAAAAQAAJ.
14. Frederick Thomas Elworthy, *The Evil Eye: An Account of This Ancient & Widespread Superstition* (London: John Murray, 1895), 129–133, 192–194, 350, 355, 360. https://books.google.com/books?id=yIdAAAAAYAAJ.
15. Marian Roalfe Cox, *Introduction to Folk-Lore* (London: David Nutt, 1897), 94. https://books.google.com/books?id=eJAHe05UBJUC.

14

※

ats and Other Beasts

Vampires and bats often go hand in hand, or hand in wing if you like. It's a connection that can certainly be found in *Dracula*. One example occurs fairly early in the book, while Mina is sharing a room with Lucy during a visit to the town of Whitby. Mina awakens during the night and sees Lucy pointing at the window. Lucy, who was suffering from sleepwalking, was not conscious while doing this. When Mina looks out the window to investigate, she states: "Between me and the moonlight flitted a great bat, coming and going in great, whirling circles."[1] The bat then flies away and Lucy returns to a restful sleep. At this point in the novel, Mina did not realize what she was really seeing—Count Dracula in the form of a bat. As the protagonists learn who and what their foe really is, they come to understand that this is one of the many supernatural abilities that Dracula possesses.

In today's popular culture, a vampire's ability to transform into a bat is a well-established trait. Additionally, the pointy ears and winglike capes often present in modern vampire imagery help cement this association. It certainly seems logical, as both vampires and bats are nocturnal, not to mention customarily feared. Plus, there's actually a type of bat that literally drinks blood from living creatures. You would think that the real-life vampire bat would have somehow influenced traditional vampire folklore. However, as we've learned in previous chapters, we must take nothing for granted. Therefore, let's take a closer look at this relationship.

Real vampire bats do indeed survive exclusively on a diet of blood that they obtain from living animals, such as cattle, chickens, and even humans. Venturing out at night, the bat will bite into its unwilling donor by using its extremely sharp teeth. It is this sharpness that allows the event to go unnoticed by the prey. Rather than sucking from the wound, the bat will lick up the blood as it flows out. An anticoagulant in the bat's saliva ensures that its meal does not end prematurely. In isolation these bites are minor injuries, but there are some serious risks: wounds can get infected, repeated attacks can weaken animals, and the bats can transmit rabies. One important thing to note is that the vampire bat is not native to Europe. Rather, this creature is only found in Latin America. The earliest European encounter with these bats occurred back in the sixteenth century.

The vampire bat's lack of presence in Europe is the first major blow to connecting them with folklore. Even though the European explorers became aware of the bats in the 1500s, it's hard to know how well information about this species would have traveled. Plus, notions of a blood-gorged undead body already existed in the Old World. For example, William of Newburgh's *sanguisuga* (discussed back in chapter 3) predates the vampire bat encounters by at least a few hundred years. It's also important to mention that prior to at least 1765, these animals weren't even known as "vampire" bats. The term was applied to them by the Comte de Buffon because of the blood-drinking trait they shared with the folkloric vampire.[2] Truth be told, there isn't much in folklore linking bats with vampires. In fact, bats were not referenced in any of the vampire tales mentioned in this book thus far. It's especially surprising given how prevalent bats are in modern vampire media and how well they seem to fit in.

However, the story isn't over yet. One tale that's certainly worth mentioning comes from the 1870 book *Vikram and the Vampire*. It's an adaptation by Sir Richard Francis Burton of an old Indian story. To briefly summarize, it involves a king named Vikram who, at the request of a sorcerer he is indebted to, must retrieve a body hanging from a tree in a cemetery. When Vikram approaches it, he finds that "it held on to a bough, like a flying fox, by the toe-tips."[3] It's also extremely thin and bloodless and has a small, goatlike tail. Vikram realizes that this body is, in fact, a "Baital," which the book then subsequently refers to as a vampire. The bulk of the book is the baital telling Vikram various stories that end in a question. Every time Vikram answers correctly, the baital escapes back up the tree and Vikram must again retrieve it.

In terms of the text, the only real connection between bats and the baital is the description of how it hangs from the tree. It doesn't actually transform into the animal or anything like that. Ernest Griset's illustrations in the book, however, paint a different picture. One image has the baital hanging from a branch and is essentially a bat with a humanoid head. Other depictions portray it as something more devil-like—it has arms and legs (with long feet), bat wings on its back, small horns, and a long tail. In the 1893 edition of the book, the bat connection is further strengthened by a new preface written by Sir Richard's wife, Isabel Burton. In it, she states, "The Baital-Pachisi, or Twenty-five Tales of a Baital, is the history of a huge Bat, Vampire, or Evil Spirit which inhabited and animated dead bodies."[4] Lady Burton's description here seems to be more in line with those illustrations. Interestingly, she also informs us that the baital is an entity residing within the corpse, rather than the corpse itself.

It's a curious connection, but it seems like the baital doesn't exactly equate to a vampire. However, referring to it as one likely helped communicate the general concept to the book's readers. A similarity to bats gets mentioned and illustrated, but that's not quite the bat transformation we're looking for.

So, does this mean that vampire folklore is entirely devoid of bat trans-formations? Well, generally speaking, that has been the prevailing wisdom.

It's been argued that Bram Stoker invented the concept when he wrote Dracula.

However, I was excited to find a recent academic paper written by Kevin Dodd, who made some fascinating discoveries in this area. Contrary to popular opinion, Dodd actually found two late-nineteenth-century literary works predating *Dracula* that include a vampire taking the form of a bat. Even more exciting, in my opinion, were two references to folkloric vampires being able to turn into bats: one from an 1879 English source and another from an 1880 German source.[5] So, although it's extremely rare, it seems that a belief in bat metamorphoses is not entirely unheard of.

Of course, it's difficult to know what Bram Stoker was aware of when he wrote *Dracula*. Plus, it seems highly likely that his book, and the subsequent adaptations thereof, are the reasons why we have vampires transforming into bats today. Although it now seems Stoker can't lay claim to being the first to introduce this trend, he certainly popularized it. I think most would agree that it's hard to imagine our vampire lore without this winged trait.

Fictional vampires aren't limited to just transforming into bats, though. In the *Dracula* novel, the count also has the ability to turn into a wolf. That was actually the form he took when his ghost ship first arrives in England: "But the strangest of all, the very instant the shore was touched, an immense dog sprang up on deck from below, as if shot up by the concussion, and running forward, jumped from the bow on the sand."[6] It certainly adds another dimension to the threat Dracula poses, but was such a thing ever truly believed? Well, this time, the folklore is a bit more generous.

You may recall that, in chapter 5, I discussed a sixteenth-century account of a shoemaker returning from the grave and tormenting the residents of Breslau. It was only by burning his corpse that the people were able to rid themselves of this vampire. Well, the shoemaker wasn't the only undead resident that these citizens had to contend with. At some point after the shoemaker's initial earthly departure, his maid also dies. Eight days later, she appears to one of the other female servants. Like some of the previous vampire tales we've discussed, the undead maid lies on top of the woman. The account states that the maid was so heavy that the woman's eyes became extremely swollen from the encounter. A number of assaults and troubles are attributed to the undead maid, including one incident where she takes the form of a hen. When one of the other maids pursues the hen, the creature grows to an immense size and grabs that woman by the throat, which remained swollen for some time after the attack. The undead maid was also believed to take the form "of a Woman, of a Dog, of a Cat, and of a Goat." After a month, her body was exhumed and burned—and the problems ceased.[7]

The maid of Breslau is an interesting case in which not only is there a dog transformation, the undead actually turns into a variety of animals. You may be surprised to learn that this sort of thing isn't unique to this story. For example, there was a Wallachian belief concerning a being known as a *murony*. When exhumed, it was thought to have some of the vampiric indicators we've found in other accounts—fingernails and toenails that had grown since death, and blood flowing from the orifices of the head. The *murony* was believed to be able to appear as "a dog, a cat, or a toad, and also of any blood-sucking insect."[8] An encyclopedia article from 1883 gets a bit more specific with the animals a vampire can turn into, listing "a dog, frog, toad, cat, flea, louse, bug, spider, [etc.]."[9] As the list of animals keeps growing, the dog is consistently included.

One last account I'd like to mention occurred at some point before 1809 in Geneva, Greece. The bishop there became aware that one of his priests had exhumed two bodies and had thrown them into the Haliacmon River. The priest had apparently believed that the corpses were vampires (*vrukolakas*). When questioned about this, the priest admitted to the deed but offered up a defense. He said that "a large animal" had been seen making a fiery exit from the grave containing those bodies. The bishop was unconvinced. He fined the priest and threatened to cut off his beard as punishment. The bishop then issued a warning to his diocese that priests performing such acts would be fined and could lose their positions. Apparently, this proved effective at ending future vampire executions.[10] Unfortunately, we don't have precise details about what kind of animal it was. Given that one wasn't specified, it may have been that the eyewitnesses weren't exactly sure. However, this still serves as a solid example of how some folkloric beliefs did include vampires taking the form of animals.

Ultimately, it seems that this investigation has reached a rather unexpected conclusion. The animal we most associate with vampires these days (namely, the bat) has an extremely limited presence in folklore—so limited it was often believed to be nonexistent. Dracula's wolf/dog form appears to have a much-stronger precedent. Plus, vampires were believed to turn into all kinds of other animals we would never consider today. However, maybe it's time for these animals to make a comeback. Maybe moviegoers would like to see a vampire goat. You never know.

※〈〈◆〉〉※

Endnotes

1. Stoker, *Dracula*, 96.
2. Comte de Buffon, *Histoire naturelle, générale et particuliére, avec la description du Cabinet du Roi*, vol. 20 (Paris: Imprimerie Royale, 1765), 74. https://books.google.com/books?id=zgI46UADVXIC.
3. Richard F. Burton, *Vikram and the Vampire, or Tales of Hindu Devilry* (London: Longmans, Green, 1870), 46. https://books.google.com/books?id=kf3nPPocKMQC.
4. Isabel Burton, "Preface to the Memorial Edition," in Richard F. Burton, *Vikram and the Vampire, or Tales of Hindu Devilry*, memorial ed., ed. Isabel Burton (London: Tylston and Edwards, 1893), xi. https://books.google.com/books?id=LXyBAAAAMAAJ.
5. Kevin Dodd, "'Blood Suckers Most Cruel': The Vampire and the Bat in and before Dracula," accessed November 20, 2017, at www.academia.edu/27682302/_Blood_Suckers_Most_Cruel_The_Vampire_and_the_Bat_in_and_before_Dracula.
6. Stoker, *Dracula*, 81.
7. More, *An Antidote against Atheism*, 214.
8. Ralston, *Russian Folk-Tales*, 325–326.
9. "Vampire," in *Chamber's Encyclopædia: A Dictionary of Universal Knowledge for the People*, vol. 9 (Philadelphia: J. B. Lippincott, 1883), 708. https://books.google.com/books?id=vZ0MAAAAYAAJ.
10. William Martin Leake, *Travels in Northern Greece*, vol. 4 (London: J. Rodwell, 1835), 216–217. https://books.google.com/books?id=k0AVtzlZky0C.

15

*

By Invitation Only

Perhaps one of the strangest traits sometimes seen in modern vampires is their inability to enter a house without first being invited.

It likely presents a number of challenges for authors and screenwriters. It essentially precludes the monster from randomly attacking people in their beds. Instead, the vampire has to schmooze his or her way in, or maybe just attack people in more-public settings. A few of the modern works to include this type of trait are the TV miniseries *Salem's Lot* (1979), the movie *The Lost Boys* (1987), and the TV series *Buffy the Vampire Slayer* (1997–2003). As one might expect, Stoker's novel also has this detail. While discussing Dracula's abilities, Van Helsing explains, "He may not enter anywhere at the first, unless there be some one of the household who bid him to come; though afterwards he can come as he please."[1] As inconvenient as this limitation is, it's well established.

At first glance, this trait certainly seems to have an air of authenticity about it. Why would a writer introduce such a serious and unexpected limitation on their antagonist? It feels more like the product of a fearful populace trying to reassure itself. Are we dealing with an authentic belief? Well, the folklore on this one was a little unexpected.

First, I want to say that I haven't been holding back this detail from any of the accounts or legends we've discussed thus far. Most tales have vampires entering homes at will and terrorizing those within. No invitation required. Given the panic that gripped some villages in Europe, this really isn't that surprising. If random people were mysteriously falling ill, an invitation-related belief would have been a bit incongruous with the events that were unfolding. However, there are some customs that must be mentioned, as they do bear a similarity to the invitation motif.

On the Greek island of Chios, it was believed that the *vrykolakas* had a rather specific pattern of behavior. It would wander through the village, normally at night, and knock on the doors to people's homes. While doing so, this creature would call out for someone who lived there. If that person were to respond to the *vrykolakas*, he or she would die the following day. Luckily, however, this vampire would only ask once. Therefore, to avoid danger, a villager would remain silent and wait for a second summons. If another was heard, the nighttime visitor could not be a vampire and it was safe to respond.[2]

Interestingly, a similar trait was also found in Romania. Although, in that country, the belief was that the vampire was limited to asking twice. So, you would have to wait for a third request before responding to a visitor. If people did reply to a vampire, the creature might then kill them. Alternatively, it may distort the person's mouth, make them unable to speak, or cut off one of their feet.[3] Given this kind of perceived threat, one wonders if villagers simply got into a habit of always asking three times the moment they started knocking.

At first glance, these beliefs from Greece and Romania may seem to confirm that invitations are a part of folklore. However, when you look closer, you can see that there are some flaws with that argument. Without a doubt, the vampire is refraining from entering someone's house and is behaving as a visitor needing admittance. It's essential to note, though, that an invitation is never actually offered. Rather, the victim simply responds to the vampire's call. It's an acknowledgment, not an invitation, which seals their fate. As such, we can't truly say this is the origin of our modern-day trope.

Let's now turn to a tale from Botoșani, Romania, that adds another dimension to this topic. It begins by telling us of an unnamed girl and young man who were in love, but, unbeknownst to the girl, the man dies. One night afterward, his vampire shows up outside her home while her parents are away. The story explains that vampires are unable to enter houses that are "clean and holy." Rather, they can go inside only those that are empty or "unclean." Because he is powerless to enter, the vampire calls to the girl at her window. Because she was unaware that he was dead, and there was nothing strange in how he spoke to her, the vampire is able to convince the girl to leave the house and accompany him. When they arrive at his tomb and he tries to get her to enter, she becomes frightened. Claiming to have lost her beads, she runs off and eventually finds a house with a light on. She enters, locks the door, and hides behind the oven. Unfortunately, inside this house is a dead man who, coincidentally, is also a vampire. When the first vampire arrives, the second vampire is about to let him in when a sympathetic hen crows (because the rooster refuses to do so!), and the girl is able to get away. The story ends by saying that the girl, herself, was "clean and holy," and those kinds of souls are hard for vampires to catch.[4]

Although this tale has a number of interesting elements, what's really relevant to our current discussion is the vampire's inability to set foot inside the girl's house. In this instance, the vampire would most likely have entered if he had been able to do so. Instead, he had to work around his limitations, just like in a modern TV show or movie. It nicely fits with our expectations, but there are issues here too. The vampire in this tale never seeks an invitation, although it's pretty clear he could have gotten one if he had asked. The story stresses that it's

the holiness of the house that's keeping the vampire out—a lack of permission is never mentioned. So, it seems safe to assume that the vampire would have been stuck outside even if the girl had asked him to come in. Also, a vampire freely entering an empty house might fit with our modern notions (as there's no one to seek an invitation from), but a vampire entering an unclean house with no invitation seems to be more of a gray area.

Ultimately, although folklore brings us rather close to the modern vampiric trait of needing an invitation, it never quite gets there. So, to find the true source of this belief, we have to look to vampire fiction. We must again turn to the literature of the nineteenth century.

I'd first like to discuss a fictional work that has not yet been covered in this book. It's a short story titled "The Mysterious Stranger." Originally written in German, its English translation was first published in the 1854 edition of *Chambers's Repository of Instructive and Amusing Tracts*. The story involves a noble family who has recently taken ownership of an estate in the Carpathian Mountains. They unwittingly play host to a local vampire that presents himself as a knight fallen on hard times and goes by the name of Azzo von Klatka. He routinely shows up in the evening for social visits, where he's rude to everyone except the patriarch's daughter, Franziska von Fahnenberg. As the days go by, she starts wasting away while Azzo seems to look healthier than before. Not to mention that Franziska is plagued by what she believes are dreams where Azzo visits her in the night and places a painful kiss upon her neck. Thankfully, a family acquaintance arrives who realizes what's going on, and is able to assist.

The story includes some emphasis on the vampire's invitation, which is certainly noteworthy. When they first speak with Azzo in a ruined church on the estate, Franziska is immediately enamored of him. She stresses that he must visit their castle, but Azzo essentially says that he isn't good company and sleeps during the day anyway. When she persists in inviting him, the vampire replies, "You wish it? You press the invitation?"[5] When Franziska then answers in the affirmative, he states,

"If my company does not please you at any time, you will have yourself to blame for an acquaintance with one who seldom forces himself, but is difficult to shake off."[6]

When the vampire does make his first social call at their home, he makes it a point to mention that he was "not uninvited."[7]

This focus on the invitation certainly gives the impression that it was important to the vampire, perhaps even essential. However, nothing more concrete is ever said about it. Also, Azzo usually behaves in a snide manner and makes a number of inside jokes about his vampiric condition. Given this, it could simply be that he took a perverse pleasure in his prey actually inviting him in. In my opinion, we can't say with complete certainty that this is the first instance of a vampire requiring an invitation in fiction.

So, where does this leave us? If "The Mysterious Stranger" left any ambiguity, where in fiction is it first and unequivocally shown that vampires must be invited? Well, it appears that we can again thank Bram Stoker. Van Helsing's quote that I gave at the beginning of the chapter leaves no room for doubt about the vampire's limitation in this regard. After going through a variety of folklore as well as an earlier nineteenth-century work, it would appear that we've come full circle.

Ultimately, this notion of vampires not being able to enter a home without an invitation seems to have evolved over time. We first had folkloric vampires knocking on doors and being barred from holy houses. We then had the fictional Azzo requiring his victim to very purposefully invite him. One naturally wonders if any of this influenced Stoker. Although it's unknown if he read "The Mysterious Stranger," there are a number of parallels between this short story and *Dracula* that are certainly compelling. However Stoker arrived at it, we end up with Van Helsing explaining this peculiar trait as if it were a piece of established canon. From there, it made its way through various adaptations into our modern perceptions, as if it had always been there.

⫷⫸

Endnotes

1. Stoker, *Dracula*, 245.
2. Bowman, *The Crimes of the Oedipodean Cycle*, 47.
3. Murgoci, "The Vampire in Roumania," 63.
4. Ibid., 70–71.
5. "The Mysterious Stranger," *Chambers's Repository of Instructive and Amusing Tracts*, vol. 8 (Edinburgh: W. and R. Chambers, 1854), no. 62, 13. https://books.google.com/books?id=MQ0bAAAAYAAJ.
6. Ibid.
7. Ibid., no. 62, 14.

16

*

Superhuman
bilities

These days, the vampires we see in films or on TV normally have all kinds of amazing abilities. Their powers are often reminiscent of what we might find in comic books or superhero movies. This certainly makes them extremely menacing, not to mention entertaining, but one does wonder how much of this is a modern development. In this chapter, I'm going to look at a number of these superhuman abilities, one by one, and attempt to discern their origins.

Super Strength

It's almost a given that any fictional vampire you watch is going to have some degree of super strength. It would be weird if a normal human out-muscled a vampire, right? With this in mind, it certainly seems likely that the folkloric vampire would share this trait with its modern, fictional counterpart. However, I actually had a hard time finding instances where traditional beliefs included vampiric super strength. These monsters are certainly dangerous and feared, but actual physical might isn't often mentioned.

One tradition that does support this belief comes from Bulgaria, which has some interesting variations in its vampire myths. In that country, it was thought a vampire would rise from the grave after being buried for nine days. However, it would only have a shadowy, incorporeal form to begin with. Its physical body would revive after forty days. Even during its ethereal stage, though, the vampire was believed to be capable of great strength. In a nineteenth-century account from Derekuoi, such a vampire grabbed the village's wrestling champion, Kodja Keraz, by the waist with force sufficient to put the man's life in danger. The vampire challenged Keraz to throw him. Luckily the champion was able to do so, but not without breaking his own jaw in the process.[1]

For one other example, we must look to the north of Europe. In Norse mythology, a *draugr* is an undead corpse with large claws, superhuman strength, and a cannibalistic appetite. These creatures can be found in or near their burial mounds, where they will wrestle with any potential grave robbers. The methods of killing a *draugr* are quite consistent with the traditions we've found elsewhere. One approach would be to sever the corpse's head and place it beneath the body. The other would be to drive a stake into the creature and burn it until only ashes remain.[2]

The vampire's superior physical strength seems to have been introduced into fiction in 1819's "The Vampyre" by John Polidori (first mentioned in chapter 2). At one point in the story, the vampire, Lord Ruthven, is described as "one whose strength seemed superhuman."[3] Given the impact that this story had on later writers, it's likely that we have Polidori to thank for a vampiric trait that we know so well today.

Flight

Sometimes our pop culture vampires can fly through air like a superhero or levitate above the ground. No bat transformation required. You see this in movies such as *The Lost Boys* (1987) and *Interview with the Vampire* (1994), as well as TV shows such as *True Blood* (2008–2014). Going back a little further, you also find it in the 1979 TV miniseries *Salem's Lot*. Upon initial consideration, this ability struck me as having a more modern feel to it. It's as if society was trying to up the ante on a monster that may have grown a little too predictable. Plus, the vampires of folklore are inherently physical in nature, so ghostlike levitation doesn't quite seem to fit.

After researching this, I found only a couple of examples of folkloric vampires with the ability to fly. I want to stress that these are vampires as I've defined them in this book. Other vampire-like creatures (such as the *penanggalan* I mentioned in chapter 1) have well-established aerial abilities.

The first account is a Russian folk tale concerning a peasant walking home with his dog one night after a day of unsuccessful hunting. When he came to a crossroads, he saw a corpse standing there in a white shroud. Although he was quite frightened, the peasant decided to proceed anyway. As he approached, the corpse started floating toward him, hovering about a foot off the ground. This creature then made a final dash at the man, but luckily the dog interceded. The animal grabbed the corpse by its ankles, and a struggle ensued. The peasant, seizing the opportunity, ran away. The fight continued until daybreak, specifically cockcrow, when the corpse then collapsed lifelessly to the ground. The dog never forgave the peasant for this abandonment, and it was ultimately killed after attacking the man.[4] This tale proves to be a rather unique example of a vampire levitating. However, if we want a more dramatic example of flight, we must set our sights past Europe.

In China, there was a belief in reanimated corpses known as *kiang shi*, which would feed upon the flesh and blood of the living. Some descriptions of these creatures include them being covered in long, white hair. They could also have extremely stiff limbs. I could also have mentioned this monster in the previous section, as they were thought to have great strength. Of course, I'm talking about the *kiang shi* now because, as I'm sure you guessed, they were believed to be able to fly through the air. One account involves a magician casting a magical net over the earth and sky to prevent the creature from flying away. The villagers, who had lost children to the monster, were now able to do battle with it. Once daylight arrived, the *kiang shi* fell lifeless to the ground and was thus burned by the people. While all this was going on, one brave villager had run into the *kiang shi*'s deep grave and continuously rang bells. This prevented the creature from retreating back into its tomb.[5]

It's at this point that you're probably wondering if nineteenth-century literature popularized the notion of flying or levitating vampires. It's certainly given us a number of other traits. Well, not this time around, I'm afraid. Flying doesn't feature in any of those major vampire-themed works. It would seem that after some isolated folkloric accounts, flying vampires took a hiatus during the 1800s. They returned again in the twentieth century and have stuck around into the twenty-first. Although it's certainly not an omnipresent trait, defying gravity seems like something vampires will keep up for a while to come.

Hypnosis

Among the strange and supernatural powers we find in pop culture vampires, one that routinely shows up is their ability to entrance or exert influence over their victims. For simplicity's sake, I'll refer to this as hypnosis. It's fairly common and can be seen in TV shows such as *Buffy the Vampire Slayer* (1997–2003) and *True Blood* (2008–2014). It's also found in such movies as *Dark Shadows* (2012), not to mention Universal's 1931 classic *Dracula*.

This trait makes the vampire a uniquely terrifying foe. How can you fight a monster when you can't even trust your own mind?

In terms of folklore, I've only run across one story that features something like this—and it's a stretch at best. There is a Russian tale where a soldier encounters the undead corpse of a warlock (I briefly mentioned this story in chapter 8). The warlock asks the soldier to join him in attending a wedding in the village. They both go and, at first, the vampire seems to be enjoying the festivities. Eventually, though, the undead guest grows angry and chases out everyone in attendance except the soldier and the newly married couple. The warlock then puts the bride and groom into a deep sleep, which allows him to make cuts on their hands and thus collect their blood in vials. Later on, the warlock explains to the solder that the couple could only be revived if their blood were returned to them via cuts made on their ankles. The warlock goes on to explain how he, himself, can be killed if his body is burned on a pile of aspen wood. He stipulates that any creatures emerging from that fire must also be slain. The vampire then attempts to kill the soldier. The soldier fights back, but it starts to look like the vampire will prevail. Thankfully, the warlock ends up being rendered lifeless by the rooster's crow at dawn. The soldier is then able to use his knowledge to save the couple and help the villagers destroy the vampire.[6]

From a certain point of view, the vampiric warlock putting the newlyweds into a deep sleep could be construed as a type of hypnotism. However, it seems unlikely he had this power because he was undead. His supernatural abilities as a warlock may have been enough, as far as folklore goes, to magically induce sleep. It seems probable that we have here an example of spell casting, rather than our popular notion of vampiric hypnosis.

So, if it wasn't folklore, what really introduced hypnosis into the vampire mainstream? Well, it would seem that this trait, or at least some sort of influence over others, is present throughout nineteenth-century literature. Starting in 1819 with Polidori's *The Vampyre*, we find Lord Ruthven, whose gaze could mysteriously cause fear and awe in those he observed. Just by a look he could "pierce through to the inward workings of the heart."[7] Additionally, this vampire had an alluring effect on women. One character describes him as having "possession of irresistible powers of seduction."[8] This may not necessarily be hypnotism as we see it in the movies, but the story certainly indicates that the vampire has a strong psychological effect on others.

If we jump to the penny dreadful *Varney the Vampire* from the 1840s, we find a vampire that has a paralyzing glare. During the first chapter, Sir Francis Varney slowly makes his way through a window, into a young woman's bedchamber. She watches in horror at his approach but is unable to make an effective cry for help or escape. The text then states: "But her eyes are fascinated. The glance of a serpent could not have produced a greater effect upon her than did the fixed gaze of those awful, metallic-looking eyes that were bent on her face."[9] It later states that she is unable to look away, and that the vampire "holds her with his glittering eye."[10] That's certainly sounding pretty hypnotic.

Of course, we find hypnotism in *Dracula* as well. The count seems to have some kind of hold over his victim Lucy Westenra, such that she sleepwalks out to meet him. We also know he is able to disorient Jonathan Harker in order to attack Jonathan's wife, Mina. Interestingly, hypnotism is actually used against the count. Because Mina had been infected by the count's vampirism, the two share a psychic link. Van Helsing is able to hypnotize Mina, such that she can provide details as to the vampire's whereabouts.

It's rather interesting that even though hypnosis is virtually nonexistent in vampire folklore, it's found in multiple nineteenth-century works. It likely fit with the suave or carnally dangerous vampires that were developing during that time. The thought of hypnotism or mesmerism may also have fascinated the minds of Victorian readers. Naturally, as with many of the traits introduced in literature, it's endured and adapted into the modern day.

Rapid Healing

You don't normally see a modern vampire with a cast on his arm or a bandage around his head. They're a pretty durable bunch and, when injured, often exhibit accelerated healing—unless the injury is a stake through the heart or something like that. A lot of folklore doesn't specifically mention this type of trait. However, because there were prescribed ways of destroying a vampire, it stands to reason that other types of assaults were believed to be ineffective.

There is actually a folkloric account that describes a vampire with an incredible healing ability. It supposedly occurred in Amărăşti, Romania, in about 1899. Some months after the death of an elderly woman, her grandchildren begin to pass away. First it's the children of her eldest son, then those of the youngest son. These two men, fearing that their deceased mother is the cause, dig up her body one night. They cut the corpse in two and then rebury it. Unfortunately, the children keep dying. The men then dig up their mother for a second time and are shocked to see that her body is back together in one piece, with no evidence of the injury they inflicted. This time, they resort to much more drastic measures. They take the corpse deep into the forest, where they disembowel it and remove the heart (which contained liquid blood). The heart is cut into four pieces and burned to ashes. Those ashes were mixed with water and given to the children to drink—a tradition you undoubtedly recall from earlier discussions in this book. Last, the body itself was burned and those ashes were buried. This extreme practice was supposedly successful, and none of the remaining children died.[11]

Weather Manipulation

This one is rather offbeat, I know. We don't normally think of vampires as being able to control the weather. It's a pretty impressive power that seems more than a little disconnected from what we would expect of a reanimated corpse. However, I'm mentioning it because this actually comes up in the *Dracula* novel. While discussing the count's abilities, Van Helsing states, "he can, within his range, direct the elements: the storm, the fog, the thunder."[12] Dracula appears to utilize these abilities while being transported to England via a ship known as the *Demeter*. Toward the end of the voyage, after a number of crewmen have mysteriously disappeared, it's implied that Dracula has created a thick fog that follows the vessel. When the ship does reach England, and no one is left alive to steer it, a sudden storm miraculously blows the *Demeter* safely into a harbor. This impressive ability was carried into the 1992 film *Bram Stoker's Dracula*.

Unlike some of the other details found in *Dracula*, such as garlic or bats, it seems that weather manipulation hasn't really thrived in modern vampire media. This may be especially surprising as there is some folkloric basis for it. In Russia, it was thought that the presence of a vampire could indeed result in storms, not to mention droughts and famines.[13] A belief in vampires causing droughts was also present in Transylvania.[14]

One particular example occurred in 1887 in the village of Ivanovka (in modern Ukraine). Shortly after a peasant had committed suicide, the entire province, known as Cherson, was afflicted by a drought. The people felt that the deceased peasant was the root of the problem. They assembled at his grave and poured water onto it while saying a prayer for rain. Unfortunately, this ritual did not produce the expected result. The body was then exhumed and reburied in a gorge past the boundaries of the village.[15] Although this might not be a traditional vampire in the sense of it making nighttime visitations, it certainly fits into the archetype of the dead causing harm to the living.

It's possible that weather manipulation fell off our vampire radar due to the way in which the monster has evolved.

Sudden droughts or floods could certainly be devastating to a small agrarian village. Just like with a mysterious plague, a frightened populace may look for a supernatural scapegoat. Thus the folkloric vampire fulfills a need here. As the literary vampire started making his home in urban cities, rubbing elbows with high society, his impact on the weather may have had less resonance with readers. Still, a dark and stormy night certainly never hurts.

Immortality

This one is really the grand prize of being a vampire. Living forever is a pretty tempting proposition—even if you do have to drink blood, avoid the sun, and essentially be a bad guy. Sometimes in movies you actually get characters that actively seek out the vampire's bite, in the hopes of becoming immortal themselves. Of course, to live out the rest of eternity forever cursed could also be the ultimate punishment. Regardless of your take on it, immortality is an almost ubiquitous aspect of our pop culture vampires.

Most traditional tales and accounts don't necessarily state that a vampire is immortal. However, it certainly seems implied. For one thing, they already died once, so it's unlikely they would die a second time from old age. In the Plogojowitz account, the villagers were afraid that the vampire would eventually kill all of them.[16] They don't specify what would have happened to the creature afterward, but they weren't about to let things get to that point. In Hungary, one suspected vampire had been dead for over thirty years before being dispatched by order of the Count de Cabreras.[17] Not exactly an eternity, but it wasn't a recent burial by any means.

If you really want a folkloric vampire with some staying power, consider Sava Savanovic of Serbia. His legend was included in the 1880 book *After Ninety Years*, written by Milovan Glišić. This vampire was believed to inhabit a watermill on the Rogacica River, in the village of Zarozje. Those who used the mill were in danger of being attacked by the undead Savanovic, who would drink their blood. Flash forward to the year 2012. The infamous watermill collapsed and some people in the village were worried that the vampire would now be in search of a new home and new victims. The story got a great deal of attention from the international press, and there were hopes that the publicity would help tourism.[18] As far as the immortality discussion goes, you have a vampire here that was believed to be in existence for, at very least, 132 years.

As we've seen numerous times before, supernatural beliefs aren't always easy to define. Such is the case with the vampire's unending state of living death. There was a belief in Romania that a vampire would continue killing villagers and livestock for a period of seven years. After this point, it would venture out into another country and become human again. This former vampire would even marry and have children. However, those offspring, upon their deaths, would become vampires themselves.[19] One particular group of Romani believed that rather than seven years, vampires had to wait thirty years for their humanity. After that, they could take up professions such as a salesman or a butcher! Other groups thought that this transformation could take three to four years or fourteen years.[20] Regardless of the time frame, the notion that a vampire would naturally become human again is quite surprising. Also, if former vampires were thought to move away, one wonders if new arrivals to a village were viewed with some suspicion.

Immortality or a return to humanity wasn't always in the cards, though. Some Romani believed that vampires simply had a limited undead lifespan. One group only had them surviving for around three months. Another group was even less generous, believing the vampires only had forty days.[21] This particular belief would certainly have provided some amount of comfort. Even if the villagers were unable to locate a suspected vampire, it wouldn't be able to torment them forever. Eventually, the threat would to cease of its own accord.

Summary

Overall, it seems we've found folkloric accounts for most of the superhuman abilities discussed in this chapter. Certainly some examples were quite obscure, but persistence often pays off when vampire hunting. With all these powers, we see how various cultures amplified the danger of the vampire. You'd think an undead corpse attacking people in the night would be scary enough. It seems likely that fear, or maybe just the desire to tell a scary story, caused the vampire to gain all kinds of amazing abilities.

Endnotes

1. St. Clair and Brophy, *A Residence in Bulgaria*, 49.
2. A. LeRoy Andrews, "Studies in the Fornaldarsqgur Norðrlanda," in *Modern Philology*, vol. 10, 1912–1913, eds. John M. Manly (Chicago: University of Chicago Press, 1913), 602–604. https://books.google.com/books?id=97cnAQAAIAAJ.
3. John William Polidori, *The Vampyre: A Tale* (London: Sherwood, 1819), 47. https://books. google.com/books?id=ZMsBAAAAQAAJ.
4. Ralston, *Russian Folk-Tales*, 317–318.
5. J. J. M. de Groot, *The Religious System of China*, vol. 5 (Leiden, The Netherlands: E. J. Brill, 1907), 745–746. https://books.google.com/books?id=lr1ZAAAAMAAJ.
6. Ralston, *Russian Folk-Tales*, 318–322.
7. Polidori, *The Vampyre: A Tale*, 28.
8. Ibid., 37.
9. Rymer or Prest, *Varney the Vampire*, chapter 1, paragraph 22.
10. Ibid., chapter 1, paragraph 23.
11. Murgoci, "The Vampire in Roumania," 50–51.
12. Stoker, *Dracula*, 242.
13. Ralston, *The Songs of the Russian People*, 410–411.
14. Gerard, "Transylvanian Superstitions," 43.
15. E. P. Evans, "Superstition and Crime," in *Appleton's Popular Science Monthly*, vol. 54, ed. William Jay Youmans (New York: D. Appleton, 1899), 214. https://books.google.com/ books?id=tJVJAAAAYAAJ.
16. Barber, *Vampires, Burial and Death*, 6.
17. Calmet, *The Phantom World*, 262–263.
18. Daily Mail Reporter, "'Put Garlic in Your Windows and Crosses in Your Homes': Serbian Council Warns Residents Vampire Is on the Loose after His 'House' Collapses," *Daily Mail*, November 27, 2012. www.dailymail.co.uk/news/article-2239072/Vampire-Sava-Savanovic-loose-Serbian-local-council-issues-public-health-warning.html;

Dragana Jovanovic, "Vampire Threat Terrorizes Serbian Village," *ABC News*, November 29, 2012. https://abcnews.go.com/International/vampire-threat-terrorizes-serbian-village/story?id=17831327;

Dusan Stojanovic, "Vampire on the Loose in Serbia?," *Daily Local News*, December 1, 2012. www.dailylocal.com/article/DL/20121201/NEWS05/121209975;

Jacob Resneck, "Serbs Hope Vampire Lore Will Scare Up Some More Tourists," *USA TODAY*, December 28, 2012. www.usatoday.com/story/news/world/2012/12/27/vampire-scare/1770213/.
19. Murgoci, "The Vampire in Roumania," 55.
20. Vukanović, "The Vampire," 238, 242–243.
21. Ibid., 242.

17

ounting

I'm sure that many people reading this book are familiar with the venerable children's program *Sesame Street*, which started airing back in 1969 and continues to this day. On that show, one of the puppet characters is a friendly, purple-skinned, Bela Lugosi-esque vampire known as Count Von Count. This curious fellow insists on counting things whenever possible, thus helping to teach the skill to children. This tendency of his clearly serves as a pun on his title. You may not think that there's anything to dive into here from a folkloric perspective, but you'd be mistaken. Surprisingly (and I have no idea if the character's creators were aware of this), there is actually a strong tradition in folklore of vampires being obsessed with counting! What were the odds? One in a million, two in a million, three in a—you get the idea.

One Greek account involves a *vrykolakas* and a man who had the distinction of being a Sabbatarian, which means he was born on a Saturday. This is quite relevant, as it was believed that anyone with that day of birth could see ghosts and have sway over vampires. This Sabbatarian was successfully able to lure the *vrykolakas* into a barn. Once inside, the monster began counting all the millet grains that were there. This gave the Sabbatarian the opportunity to nail the vampire to a wall, thus defeating it.[1]

Millet isn't the only material that vampires might be interested in counting. One Greek custom was to scatter mustard seeds over the roof so that vampires would get distracted before they had a chance to enter the house.[2] There was also a Kashubian practice of using sand or poppy seeds. They could either be placed in a bag that would go into the coffin or be scattered along the path to the grave. As before, the vampire would then be obliged to count these grains and would thus never reach its intended destination. This tallying process could take even longer than you might expect, as some people believed the vampire was limited to counting just a single grain per year.[3]

This counting phenomenon isn't exclusive to Europe, either. In India, there was a belief in beings known as *churel*, which were spirits of women who had died either while pregnant, while giving birth, or during menstruation. Although a *churel* can take different forms, such as a beautiful woman, it always has feet that point backward. The *churel* was thought to lure young men away to some otherworldly realm. If a man then ate the food there, the *churel* would prevent him from leaving until he became elderly. It was also thought that anyone who saw this being would likely suffer from some kind of wasting disease. Additionally, the *churel* was believed to rise from the grave at night and visit the friends she had in life. A way to prevent this from happening was to scatter mustard seeds over the place where she had died and along the road to the grave. One reason for doing this was that the smell of mustard blossoms was thought to sooth the ghost. The other reason, like in Europe, was that the *churel* would have to pick up all the seeds and thus get distracted until morning. She would then have to return to her grave.[4]

It's also interesting to note that there were some other rationales for scattering grains. In Romania, millet might be placed in the coffin or even in the mouth and nose of the suspected vampire. It was believed that the vampire would eat all the millet and thus be delayed for a number of days.[5] In Ukraine, salt would be scattered in a room of the house, but the vampire wouldn't be counting or eating it. Rather, this salt would allow for the vampire's footsteps to be tracked for the purpose of identifying its grave.[6]

The vampire's compulsive behavior doesn't end with counting, though. Sometimes, knots were a focus for its obsession,

as is evident in the Kashubian practice of putting a net into the coffin. The vampire would be compelled to untie all the knots before rising from the grave. Just like with the counting, some people believed that a vampire could only address one knot per year, so this method bought the village a great deal of time.[7] A similar idea is presented in a Romanian tale where a woman escapes from a vampire by using linen to plug up the entrance to its grave. The rationale for this is presumed to be that the vampire would have to untangle all the strands of fabric before proceeding.[8]

A really unusual and very specific vampire compulsion was found in Romani tradition, as well as in Serbian and Albanian beliefs. To deal with a suspected vampire, its left sock would be removed and filled with dirt from beneath the corpse's head. This sock would then be thrown into a neighboring village. It was believed that the vampire would go to retrieve this stolen property. The hope was that the monster would accidentally drown while doing so.[9] As far as folklore goes, this has to be one of the most unique ways to deal with a vampire.

So, why is it that vampires are so fanatical about counting? It's probably one of the most curious aspects of the undead in folklore. Unfortunately, I haven't been able to find a definitive answer—but I've made a few small strides. At one point, I ran across a belief in which those who deliberately spill salt and don't try to gather it up would be forced to pick up salt grains with their eyelids in the afterlife.[10] This sounds pretty intense. I started wondering if vampires might be suffering from some kind of similar spiritual punishment. It's an interesting notion, but I don't think that's quite it.

It's important to realize that this counting fixation isn't isolated to vampires. Witches were thought to suffer from the same compulsion, so they were also vulnerable to scattered seeds and other such preventives.[11] There have also been beliefs that wizards, like vampires, were compelled to untie knots.[12] Writer Charles Godfrey Leland asserted that the witch's counting was an outgrowth of the folk belief that the evil eye could be counteracted by artwork consisting of complex patterns (such as those found in Celtic designs). Witches were compelled to trace out such intricate patterns, and their gazes would thus become distracted or overwhelmed.[13] I'm not sure if this necessarily explains everything for vampires, but it certainly brings us a bit closer to understanding. With this in mind, one wonders if the vampire's obsession is really just an inherited trait from one supernatural being to another.

Of course, when you take a step back, many of the vampire's main activities, such as drinking blood and strangling people, seem to be compulsions.

It's not like the person was doing these things when they were alive—at least, hopefully not. So why are they now, in death, so compelled to torment their family and neighbors? It would seem that vampires were understood to follow a variety of rules, some more clear than others. These rules allowed for sudden illnesses to be explained, and provided people with a means of dealing with these situations—even if those methods were purely a placebo.

Counting likely never caught on in fiction because it didn't suit the suave, Victorian vampire. Can you imagine Dracula stooping over to pick up a bunch of seeds? That would certainly undercut his image and the threat he posed. The humorous nature of a vampire compulsively counting was used to great effect in a season 5 episode of the TV show *The X-Files*, titled "Bad Blood." Beyond that, it seems unlikely that counting will ever make a big comeback. However, it's ironic that for those of us who grew up with *Sesame Street*, it was the first thing we saw a vampire character doing. No word yet on the folkloric authenticity of monsters that ravenously eat baked goods.

Endnotes

1. G. F. Abbot, *Macedonian Folklore* (Cambridge, UK: Cambridge University Press, 1903), 221. https://books.google.com/books?id=QKZZAAAAMAAJ.

2. Ibid., 219.

3. Perkowski, *Vampire Lore*, 221.

4. W. Crooke, *The Popular Religion and Folk-Lore of Northern India*, vol. 1 (Westminster, UK: Archibald Constable, 1896) 269–273. https://books.google.com/books?id=CjDXAAAAMAAJ.

5. Murgoci, "The Vampire in Roumania," 55.

6. Ralston, *Russian Folk-Tales*, 325.

7. Perkowski, *Vampire Lore*, 221.

8. Murgoci, "The Vampire in Roumania," 71.

9. Vukanović, "The Vampire," 249.

10. Abbot, *Macedonian Folklore*, 103.

11. Cross, "Witchcraft in North Carolina," 282–283; Charles Godfrey Leland, *Etruscan Roman Remains in Popular Tradition* (London: T. Fisher Unwin, 1892), 337. https://books.google.com/books?id=zaFJAAAAMAAJ.

12. Abbot, *Macedonian Folklore*, 170.

13. Leland, *Etruscan Roman Remains in Popular Tradition*, 168–170, 337.

18

alf-Vampires

$\mathfrak{E}$**very now and then in modern media, you'll find a supernatural character that's not fully human, but not fully vampire.**

They exist in an in-between state where they may possess some, but not necessarily all, of the customary vampiric qualities. These creatures can often be the result of a union between a human mother and a vampire father, though that's not always how the storyline goes. Movies that feature half-vampires include the *Blade* film series (1998, 2002, 2004) as well as the *BloodRayne* movies (2005, 2007, 2011). In both cases, the plot centers on a half-vampire that is out to destroy evil, full-blooded vampires. Interestingly, neither of the main characters (Blade and Rayne, respectively) was invented for the movies. Instead, Blade is based on the Marvel Comics character, while *BloodRayne* is a video game franchise. For one more example, there's the 1985 animated film *Vampire Hunter D*, from Japan. This movie, along with its 2000 sequel, features a half-vampire named D whose goal, as the title would imply, is to hunt down vampires. In this case, the movies were based on novels. Hybrid beings add an interesting layer of complexity to the established vampire patterns, as these characters must often come to terms with their dual natures.

I had often wondered if half-vampires were a genuine folk belief or if they were just the product of imaginative authors. The whole notion did seem a bit convenient—a way to create a superpowered yet sympathetic main character. When I first ran across confirmation that half-vampires were indeed a thing, I was pleasantly surprised. When discussing these beings, Raymond T. McNally explains that vampires were believed to be able to have children with humans, but the resulting offspring would be born without bones.[1] This additional fact was a bit of a letdown, as bones seem necessary for doing pretty much anything, especially vampire hunting. Although this extreme calcium deficiency seems strange, it actually fits with other folklore. There were some beliefs that regular vampires were boneless,[2] so it may simply be that this trait carried over into the children.

I also found reference to these boneless half-vampires in Prof. Vukanović's article about vampires in Romani cultures. However, this source also provides a whole other set of beliefs concerning this topic. It was thought that a male vampire would return to sleep with his widow or, if he had been a bachelor, any desirable woman. The resulting offspring were known by a number of names, sometimes varying based on gender: *dhampir* (m), *dhampiresa* (f), *vampir* (m), *vampiresa* (f), *vampiric*, *vampijerovic*, and *lampijerovic*. Unlike their movie counterparts, these *dhampirs* are essentially human, lacking the standard vampire traits and powers. However, unlike normal people, they do have the ability to see vampires (which would normally be invisible). Also, and most importantly, *dhampirs* can destroy vampires, and they were often employed to do so. Interestingly, this skill could be inherited, so you may be dealing with a *dhampir* that is actually generations removed from the original vampire.[3] Rev. Henry

Fanshawe Tozer, in his book on Turkey and the surrounding areas, mentions that there were a number of families in the city of Perlepe that were descended from *vrykolakas*. They were widely known for being able to dispatch vampires and would even get requests to do so from people in other cities. Apparently, they kept their methods quite secret, and people didn't socialize with them.[4]

Half-vampires, or *dhampirs*, provide further evidence of the physical nature of vampires. The undead were close enough to life that they experienced the same carnal urges and could actually father living children. That those children would then become vampire hunters makes for an interesting twist, as the vampires create their own destroyers. It's a rather unique aspect to vampire lore and, as we've seen, has endured in popular culture.

-«‹◆›»-

Endnotes

1. McNally, "Interview with the Vampire Expert," in *Dracula: Truth and Terror*.
2. Vukanović, "The Vampire," 237.
3. Ibid., 244–245, 247, 250–251, 254.
4. Henry Fanshawe Tozer, *Researches in the Highlands of Turkey: Including Visits to Mount Ida, Athos, Olympus, and Pelion, to the Mirdite Albanians, and Other Remote Tribes*, vol. 2 (London: John Murray, 1869) 90–91. https://books.google.com/books?id=vFxCAAAAcAAJ.

19

Aristocratic

These days, vampires are often depicted as being aristocratic or well-to-do. Think of Bela Lugosi's classic portrayal of Count Dracula, with his white-tie attire and suave demeanor—not to mention the noble title. It allows for an alluring vampire that can draw victims close. Given all the tales discussed in this book, I think it will come as no surprise to you that aristocratic vampires are in no way the norm in folklore. By and large, vampires were ordinary members of the community who had passed away. In life, they were villagers with jobs and families. They weren't mysterious noblemen locked away in foreboding castles. Of course, if you've ever watched any documentaries about vampires, you may have heard that Count Dracula was based on a real, historic prince, Vlad the Impaler. This may seem like a prime example of an aristocratic vampire, but we need to take a closer look.

Vlad the Impaler (1431–1476) was the *voivode* (prince) of Wallachia, a principality that now composes part of Romania. He is sometimes referred to as Vlad III, Vlad Tepes ("Tepes" being Romanian for "the Impaler"), and Vlad Dracula. This last name comes from his father, Vlad II Dracul. Vlad II was a member of the Order of the Dragon and thus had the sobriquet of "Dracul," meaning "dragon." Because of this, Vlad III was known as "Dracula," meaning "son of the dragon." It's curious to note that "dracul" can also be translated as "devil." With rebellious nobles, powerful Hungary in the north, and the threat of Ottoman invasion from the south, Vlad III's position was a precarious one. He had to struggle to achieve and maintain his throne and thus reigned as *voivode* three separate times. While ruling the country, Vlad became known for his extreme brutality, with torture and cruel executions having been attributed to him. As his Tepes title would imply, he had tens of thousands of people impaled on pikes during his reign. In modern times, Vlad has taken on the status of a national hero in Romania—someone who fought to defend his country.

The thing is, although Vlad was incredibly violent, no one in his time ever thought that he was an actual vampire. Some scholars have asserted that a contemporary poem, written by Michel Beheim, described Vlad as eating bread that he had dipped into the blood of his victims. However, Dracula scholar Dr. Elizabeth Miller states that this was a mistranslation, and the poem actually had Vlad washing his hands in the blood.[1] Disturbing? Yes. Vampiric? No.

In Stoker's novel, a link between the fictional Dracula and the historical one is clearly made with the following line from Van Helsing: "He must, indeed, have been that Voivode Dracula, who won his name against the Turk, over the great river on the very frontier of Turkey-land."[2] Was Stoker inspired by Vlad's gruesome legacy, such that the author turned the prince into a vampire? A great deal of conjecture has been made about this, but Dr. Miller describes what is known for certain.

According to Bram Stoker's notes, he found a reference to the real Dracula in an 1820 book titled *An Account of the Principalities of Wallachia and Moldavia*, written by William Wilkinson. The book says very little about Dracula. It mainly mentions some of his military endeavors and also provides a footnote stating that "Dracula" means "devil," along with some information on why the term was applied. It never discusses Dracula's proclivity for impaling, nor does it even provide his first name. This book is the only confirmed source Stoker had regarding Vlad. His use of anything else, such as other books or personal discussions, is only speculation. Miller argues that given the novel's lack of details regarding Dracula's past, it makes sense that it was Wilkinson's book alone that provided Stoker with his information on the *voivode*.[3]

With all that said, it's clear that Vlad III Dracula was never believed to be an aristocratic vampire. Even the link between the real Dracula and the fictional one is quite limited. However, it seems that the two will be forever paired.

Of course, it's certainly not impossible for folklore to have a vampire coming from the upper echelons of society, but it's quite rare. You may recall that earlier in this book we discussed a Russian governor who became a vampire and terrorized his former wife. Given his job, he could certainly be considered upper class, perhaps aristocratic depending on the time and place.

For a more clear-cut example, let's turn to a newspaper article from 1875. It tells a story concerning Nicholas Boralajova, a Serbian nobleman who had recently died while living in Paris. In his home country, it was believed that he was destined to become a vampire after death—a fate that always befell the eldest son in his family. Due to this tradition, he was forced to move abroad. The article writer dismisses the belief as superstition but stresses that this well-educated nobleman believed it. Boralajova supposedly requested that his heart be removed after death in order to avoid his vampiric fate. The article doesn't state whether his wish was honored.[4]

The notion of aristocratic vampires was likely cemented in nineteenth-century literature. Even before Count Dracula, you had a whole cast of upper-crust undead. To start things off, there was Lord Ruthven in Polidori's *The Vampyre*, from 1819. You then had Sir Francis Varney from the penny dreadful *Varney the Vampire* (1845–1847). The undead Azzo von Klatka identifies himself as a knight in the short story "The Mysterious Stranger," from 1854. I'll also mention the title character from Sheridan Le Fanu's 1872 novella, *Carmilla*, who was a vampiric countess. Gothic literature favored these blue-blooded bloodsuckers, and why not? Being aristocratic adds to the mystery and allure of the characters. Plus, it makes these vampires even more dangerous, as they're able to command respect and infiltrate high society. Simply put, it makes for a good story! It's an element that's well established, and with the immortal grip of Count Dracula on our modern notions, I doubt it will ever go away.

⫸⫷◆⫸⫷

Endnotes

1. David B Dickens and Elizabeth Miller, "Michel Beheim, German *Meistergesang*, and Dracula," *Journal of Dracula Studies* 5 (2003), posted at "Journal of Dracula Studies Archives," Kutztown University English Department, PDF, 7–8. https://kutztownenglish. files.wordpress.com/2015/09/jds_v5_2003_dickens_and_miller.pdf.
2. Stoker, *Dracula*, 246.
3. Elizabeth Miller, "Filing for Divorce: Count Dracula vs Vlad Tepes," in *Dracula: The Shade and the Shadow*, ed. Elizabeth Miller (Westcliff-on-Sea, UK: Desert Island Books, 1998), posted at Dracula's Homepage, 2005, www.ucs.mun.ca/~emiller/divorce.html.
4. "Existing Superstitions," *Andrew County Republican* (Savannah, MO), March 12, 1875. Accessed on Chronicling America: Historic American Newspapers, Library of Congress, http://chroniclingamerica.loc.gov/lccn/sn85034076/1875-03-12/ed-1/seq-6/.

20

❧

Witches and Werewolves

Vampires, witches, and werewolves are all horror staples. They're an essential part of Halloween imagery, and it's not uncommon to find movies and TV series that feature some combination of the three. How exactly these characters relate to each other can vary, but a climactic fight scene can often be in the cards. Of course, even if they are sharing screen time, they're normally portrayed as distinct supernatural beings with their own specific strengths and weaknesses. Audiences are probably pretty comfortable fitting these three monsters into separate boxes—but things are a little less straightforward in folklore. While doing research for this book, I was surprised to find a variety of instances where vampire lore overlapped with beliefs concerning both werewolves and witches. In this chapter, we'll explore these similarities and thus get a better sense of how folkloric vampires fit into a wider supernatural world.

We have already seen an example of this overlap in chapter 13, where silver bullets were effective against witches, werewolves, and, to a lesser extent, vampires.

This is in no way an isolated case. In fact, some beliefs have these creatures quite dependent on each other. For example, in parts of eastern Europe, it was thought that a vampire was born of "an unholy union between a witch and a werewolf or a devil."[1] A different belief held that witches, wizards, and werewolves would become vampires after they died.[2] Additionally, there are tales where witches turn people into werewolves.[3] Clearly, these creatures were not mutually exclusive in the folklore of a region.

With this overall thought in mind, let's take a closer look at folkloric witches—specifically their evolution in Slavic regions. Notions of the malevolent spell caster likely came about during the period of conversion to Christianity. In pagan times, there were people who were believed to have special, supernatural-related knowledge. They could help bring good weather, ensure changing seasons, and divine the future. Normally, they were important and well-respected members of the community. However, as Christianity was introduced, the old magical belief system was denounced as evil, and its practitioners were vilified. Thus the malicious witch was born.[4]

Some of the most significant overlap between witches and vampires can be found in Romanian folklore. The terms *strigoi* (masculine) and *strigoica* (feminine) are actually used to mean either entity. The way to differentiate between them would be to specify whether the *strigoi* is living or dead. It was believed that the dead variety would teach spells to the living ones. Interestingly, both kinds were thought to have an aversion to garlic. When a living *strigoi* would die, it would then continue on as a dead one.[5] Essentially, a vampire was a kind of second phase in a witch's overall existence.

Striking commonalities can also be found in William Kingston's discussion on Portuguese witches, known as *bruxas*. He describes them as women who have made a pact with evil, signed in blood. Although they will live normal lives during the day, including getting married and having children, nighttime is another matter. While everyone is asleep, the *bruxa* will rise and transform into an owl or large bat. In this form, she will fly about and fatally suck the blood of infants. Shockingly, even the *bruxa*'s own children will meet this fate, as she is unable to resist this dark compulsion. However, it's clear that some of her offspring must be spared, as it's also mentioned that the daughter of a *bruxa* may become one herself. At dawn, the *bruxa* returns home and no one realizes she was gone.[6] Kingston likens these *bruxas* to vampires, and it's not surprising why. The blood sucking is an undisputable overlap. Plus, as we've discussed, animal transformation is an established vampire trait.

In terms of shared weaknesses, there are more in folklore than the garlic and silver already discussed. You'll recall in chapter 17 that witches, in addition to vampires, suffer from a counting compulsion. For example, a tradition existed in Silesia where a small birch tree would be affixed above the front door. The witch would be unable to enter the house until she had counted every leaf. While performing this task, the sun would eventually rise and she would become powerless.[7] This notion of the rising sun dispelling the witch may also remind us of the tales where vampires became lifeless at dawn. This would appear to be yet another overlap.

As with vampires, witches could also be vulnerable to holy objects and imagery. In Silesia, three crosses would be drawn on doors in chalk to prevent witches from entering.[8] In England, a variety of sanctified items could protect people against witchcraft—specifically holy water, consecrated salt, holy candles, and blessed leaves from Palm Sunday.[9] This is probably the least surprising commonality, given that it relates to the power of good over evil.

Interestingly, the similarities don't end there. Some of the other more obscure vampire lore also matches witchcraft beliefs. Previously, it was discussed how water could be a barrier to vampires. Witches had the same kind of issue, as they weren't able to cross running streams.[10] Also, just like vampires, witches were believed to float (and thus immersion in water was used as a test for suspected witches).[11] You may recall too that vampires were believed to negatively affect the weather. This was also a trait of witches—specifically that they could create storms and droughts.[12] It would seem that the more you dig, the more things get murky between the two.

Werewolves also serve as an interesting parallel to the vampire. The notion of a man turning into a wolf can be found as far back as classical mythology. In Ovid's *Metamorphoses*, there is a tale where Zeus visits the palace of Lycaon, King of Arcadia. The king, skeptical of his guest's divinity, underhandedly sets before Zeus a meal of cooked human flesh. Zeus immediately knows the truth and punishes the tyrannical king by turning him into a wolf.[13] In this pagan case, the transformation was a punishment for transgressions. During the Middle Ages, however, the Christian perspective aligned werewolves with witchcraft and evil.[14] Witches might choose to turn into wolves or curse others by transforming them into these beasts.[15] You may recall that vampires were also believed to turn into dogs—so the very act of transformation, iconic to the werewolf, could also be considered vampiric.

One overlap you're probably expecting me to mention is the infectious bite of both werewolves and vampires. In the movies, you usually become a werewolf by getting attacked by one (and surviving). Well, surprisingly, this particular detail does not seem to be present in folklore. Instead, magic is a well-established cause—whether it's due to a witch, a ritual, or a magical item.[16] There are, however, a few other causes that bear some resemblance to the vampire origins discussed in chapter 7. For example, it was mentioned in that chapter that the seventh son or daughter in a family would become a vampire. In one part of Germany, it was thought that having seven daughters would result in one of them being a werewolf. However, the tradition did not specify which daughter it would be.[17] You may also recall chapter 7 stating that some people were simply destined to be vampires, without any specific cause. In southern France, this fateful explanation was applied to werewolves.[18] As with vampires, it would seem that the causes of lycanthropy (the condition of turning into a wolf) could vary from place to place.

The line between vampires and werewolves can actually become quite blurred in some folklore. There was a belief in Normandy that a werewolf (known in French as a *loup-garou*) could actually originate from a corpse. The body would begin by consuming the shroud on its face, and then moaning noises would be heard from the grave. Finally, a wolf would dramatically erupt out of the ground. The rationale for why this would happen was that the person's soul had been condemned.[19] This lore bears a striking resemblance to certain vampire beliefs we've discussed previously. The only real difference is that the undead ends up solely as a wolf.

As you dig, you'll find all kinds of interesting connections between these mythical monsters. Some lore held that an aspen stake was effective against werewolves as well as vampires.[20] In certain places, eating meat from a lamb that was killed by a wolf could turn a person into a vampire.[21] Even the etymology gets a little murky. One proposed origin for the term "vampire" is that it comes from *uber*, a northern Turkish word for "witch."[22] The Greek vampire term *vrykolaka* may be derived from *vukodlak*, a Serbian word meaning "wolf hairy."[23] In some Romanian lore, the *vârcolac* is a creature that eats the moon and can be translated as "werewolf."[24] One gets the sense that these entities have been influencing each other for a very long time.

One final overlap I'll discuss, and it's probably the most troubling one, relates to the ultimate way in which to destroy a vampire. Back in chapter 4, we discussed that as a final resort, a frightened populace may burn a suspected vampire corpse to ashes. Given that the undead menace was normally just a dead body, one could argue that this measure was essentially victimless. Sadly, the same cannot be said for witches. From the sixteenth century all the way into the early nineteenth century, people were accused and executed for witchcraft. It has been estimated that tens of thousands were burned alive.[25] Accusations of transforming into an animal could also end in death by burning. It's been asserted that hundreds of people were victims of this.[26] It's these kinds of events where the real dangers of superstition become clear. Fear and misunderstanding no doubt played a major role in such actions. Based on the time, place, and circumstances, it seems the finger of blame could fall on the dead or, tragically, the living.

Blood drinking, bats, garlic, and so on—it starts to get hard to find traits that are exclusively within the domain of the vampire. Even being dead isn't a foolproof indication. The various similarities we've seen among vampires, witches, and werewolves demonstrate the fluid nature of folklore. Beliefs can change, splinter, and amalgamate over time, with one set of beliefs influencing another. The vampire doesn't exist in isolation. Rather, this monster is part of a complex, and sometimes quite frightening, system of beliefs. When it comes to these supernatural traditions, absolutes can be difficult to find.

⋘⋙

Endnotes

1. Ralston, *The Songs of the Russian People*, 409–410.
2. Ibid., 409.
3. Kelly, *Curiosities of Indo-European Tradition and Folk-Lore*, 263–265.
4. Ralston, *The Songs of the Russian People*, 415–417.
5. Murgoci, "The Vampire in Roumania," 47, 56–57, 61–62.
6. William H. G. Kingston, S. E. De Morgan, Martin Doyle, et al., "The Vampire; or, Pedro Pacheco and the Bruxa," in *Tales for All Ages* (London: Bickers & Bush, 1863), 72–74. https://books.google.com/books?id=XwgGAAAAQAAJ.
7. J. G. Frazer, *The Golden Bough: A Study in Magic and Religion*, vol. 9, 3rd ed. (London: Macmillan, 1913), 162. https://books.google.com/books?id=lNM3AQAAMAAJ.
8. Ibid., 162.
9. "Witchcraft," in *Encyclopædia of Superstitions, Folklore, and the Occult Sciences of the World*, vol. 3, eds. Cora Linn Daniels and C. M. Stevens (Milwaukee, WI: J. H. Yewdale & Sons, 1903), 1453. https://books.google.com/books?id=ns0gK0efOvYC.
10. Ibid., 1446.
11. Ibid., 1447, 1449, 1451.
12. Ibid., 1449, 1455.
13. Ovid, *The Metamorphoses of Ovid*, vol. 1, trans. Henry T. Riley (Philadelphia: David McKay, 1899), 25–26. https://books.google.com/books?id=W4YXAAAAIAAJ.
14. Cox, *Introduction to Folk-Lore*, 128.
15. Sabine Baring-Gould, *The Book of Were-wolves: Being an Account of a Terrible Superstition* (London: Smith, Elder, 1865), 79, 116. https://books.google.com/books?id=m4EAAAAAMAAJ.
16. Ibid., 113, 116–117.
17. Ibid., 113.
18. Ibid., 105.
19. Ibid., 107–108.
20. Ralston, *The Songs of the Russian People*, 406.
21. Tozer, *Researches in the Highlands of Turkey*, 83–84.
22. Summers, *Vampires and Vampirism*, 18;
"Vampire," in *The New International Encyclopædia*, vol. 23, *Valjean–Zyrians*, 2nd ed., eds. Daniel C. Gilman, Harry T. Peck, and Frank M. Colby (New York: Dodd, Mead, 1917), 8. https://books.google.com/books?id=kIxIAQAAMAAJ.
23. Tozer, *Researches in the Highlands of Turkey*, 82.
24. Murgoci, "The Vampire in Roumania," 64–66.
25. Joseph Haydn, *Dictionary of Dates, and Universal Reference*, 2nd ed. (London: Edward Moxon, 1844), 554. https://books.google.com/books?id=riU-AAAAYAAJ.
26. Cox, *Introduction to Folk-Lore*, 128.

Conclusion

Before embarking on this project, I knew that there were going to be some big differences between the vampires that haunt folklore and those that inhabit popular culture. However, even with that expectation, I was quite surprised at some of the things I learned (the lack of fangs comes to mind). Additionally, the variation within folklore was fascinating. Depending on the time, place, and people, all sorts of vampire details could differ—even seemingly fundamental ones, such as how to destroy such creatures. When it comes to supernatural beliefs, there's a rich tradition to explore.

Ultimately, when we look at vampires as a whole (both fiction and folklore), I think they provide us with an interesting insight into ourselves. Back in chapter 10, I discussed how mirrors relate to vampires. Well, perhaps vampires, themselves, function as a sort of cultural mirror—reflecting fears of the era.

The differences we see between folklore and fiction may be explained by the shifting perspectives of society.

Many of the early vampire accounts we learned about, such as the Peter Plogojowitz case, were rooted in people's misunderstandings and fear. They were searching to provide some sort of explanation for events that they had no real control over, such as diseases or unexplained deaths. If the people could identify the source of the misfortune and stop it, their safety and survival could be ensured. The folkloric vampire served this purpose and likely provided some form of reassurance for a frightened populace.

In modern times, with the advantages of technology and medical science, we live in a world with a lot fewer uncertainties. By and large, the folkloric vampire has no purpose these days. However, the vampire of fiction is a very different beast. Oftentimes, there is now an emphasis on the vampire's immortality and permanent youth. Perhaps these new vampires reflect our own uneasiness with the aging process and the fear of death. These, of course, are things that science has yet to conquer. The vampire's gifts come at a price, though. Could that be an acknowledgment that nature's course should not be subverted?

With all that said, the folkloric vampire may not be fully laid to rest. In 2004, a vampire destruction ritual was carried out in the village of Marotinul de Sus, Romania. Six villagers exhumed the body of Petre Toma, a seventy-six-year-old man who had died the previous December. A pitchfork was used to extract his heart, and his body was impaled with stakes and sprinkled with garlic. The heart was then burned and mixed with water. Just as we've discussed in previous chapters, this drink was given to those who were believed to be ill as a result of the vampire's visits. In this case, the sufferers all apparently recovered. Interestingly, this was not an isolated occurrence, and other such exhumations have reportedly taken place in the region.[1] It's quite surprising that these practices can still be found in the twenty-first century, but it's a testament to the power and endurance of supernatural beliefs.

With everything we've learned about vampire accounts, traditions, fiction, and film, I think one thing is abundantly clear—the vampire's greatest power lies in its adaptability. This monster has evolved over generations to meet whatever society needed from it. Whether it's escapism or scapegoating, the vampire is there. It resonates with us on a fundamental level. It's scary, but it's also captivating, and we just can't seem to look away.

Endnote

1. Monica Petrescu, "The Long Shadow of Dracula," *The Telegraph*, February, 6, 2005. www.telegraph.co.uk/news/worldnews/europe/romania/1482941/The-long-shadow-of-Dracula.html.

Bibliography

Abbot, G. F. *Macedonian Folklore.* Cambridge, UK: Cambridge University Press, 1903. https://books.google.com/books?id=QKZZAAAAMAAJ.

Acten-mäßige und Umständliche Relation von denen Vampiren oder Menschen-Saugern. Leipzig: Augusto Martini, 1732. https://books.google.com/books?id=etRZAAAAcAAJ.

Andrews, A. LeRoy. "Studies in the Fornaldarsqgur Norðrlanda." In *Modern Philology.* Vol. 10, *1912–1913.* Edited by John M. Manly, 601–30. Chicago: University of Chicago Press, 1913. https://books.google.com/books?id=97cnAQAAIAAJ.

Barber, Paul. *Vampires, Burial and Death: Folklore and Reality.* New Haven, CT: Yale University Press, 2010.

Baring-Gould, Sabine. *The Book of Were-wolves: Being an Account of a Terrible Superstition.* London: Smith, Elder, 1865. https://books.google.com/books?id=m4EAAAAAMAAJ.

Bell, Michael E. *Food for the Dead: On the Trail of New England's Vampires.* New York: Carroll & Graff, 2001.

Blavatsky, H. P. *Isis Unveiled: A Master-Key to the Mysteries of Ancient and Modern Science and Theology.* Vol. 1. 6th ed. New York: J. W. Bouton, 1892. https://books.google.com/books?id=ca70UR08tOoC.

Blunt, Mrs. John Elijah. *The People of Turkey: Twenty Years' Residence among Bulgarians Greeks, Albanians, Turks, and Armenians.* Vol. 2. Edited by Stanley Lane Poole. London: John Murray, 1878. https://books.google.com/books?id=sZj2tM-iUlUC.

Bowman, Henry Newpher. *The Crimes of the Oedipodean Cycle.* Boston: Richard G. Badger, 1918. https://books.google.com/books?id=iLhHAAAAIAAJ.

Buffon, Comte de. *Histoire naturelle, générale et particuliére, avec la description du Cabinet du Roi.* Vol. 20. Paris: Imprimerie Royale, 1765. https://books.google.com/books?id=zgI46UADVXIC.

Burton, Isabel. "Preface to the Memorial Edition." In *Vikram and the Vampire, or Tales of Hindu Devilry.* Memorial ed. By Richard F. Burton. Edited by Isabel Burton, xi–xii. London: Tylston and Edwards, 1893. https://books.google.com/books?id=LXyBAAAAMAAJ.

Burton, Richard F. *Vikram and the Vampire, or Tales of Hindu Devilry.* London: Longmans, Green, 1870. https://books.google.com/books?id=kf3nPPocKMQC.

Calmet, Augustine. *The Phantom World: The History and Philosophy of Spirits, Apparitions, &c. &c.* 2 vols. Translated by Henry Christmas. Philadelphia: A. Hart, 1850. https://books.google.com/books?id=Z1GqcY9ow3QC.

Campbell, John Gregorson. *Witchcraft & Second Sight in the Highlands and Islands of Scotland: Tales and Traditions Collected Entirely from Oral Sources.* Glasgow: James MacLehose and Sons, 1902. https://books.google.com/books?id=shnXAAAAMAAJ.

Conway, Moncure Daniel. *Demonology and Devil-Lore.* Vol. 1. London: Chatto and Windus, 1879. https://books.google.com/books?id=Ck_OAAAAMAAJ.

"Copia eines Schreibens aus dem Gradisker District in Ungarn." *Wienerisches Diarium* (Vienna, Austria), July 21, 1725. http://anno.onb.ac.at/cgi-content/anno?aid=wrz&datum=17250721&zoom=33.

Cox, David. "Vampires, Ghosts, and Demons: The Nightmare of Sleep Paralysis." *The Guardian,* October 30, 2015. www.theguardian.com/science/blog/2015/oct/30/vampires-ghosts-and-demons-the-nightmare-of-sleep-paralysis.

Cox, Marian Roalfe. *Introduction to Folk-Lore.* London: David Nutt, 1897. https://books.google.com/books?id=eJAHe05UBJUC.

Crooke, W. *The Popular Religion and Folk-Lore of Northern India.* Vol. 1. Westminster, UK: Archibald Constable, 1896. https://books.google.com/books?id=CjDXAAAAMAAJ.

Cross, Tom Peete. "Witchcraft in North Carolina." In *Studies in Philology*. Vol. 16. Edited by Edwin Greenlaw, William M. Dey, and George Howe, 217–88. Chapel Hill: University of North Carolina Press, 1919. https://books.google.com/books?id=m65JAAAAYAAJ.

D'Argens, Marquis. *The Jewish Spy: Being a Philosophical, Historical, and Critical Correspondence, by Letters, Which Lately Passed between Certain Jews in Turkey, Italy, France, &c.* 3rd ed. Vol. 4. London: A. Millar, 1766. https://books.google.com/books?id=vXEYAAAAYAAJ.

Daily Mail Reporter. "'Put Garlic in Your Windows and Crosses in Your Homes': Serbian Council Warns Residents Vampire Is on the Loose after His 'House' Collapses." *Daily Mail*, November 27, 2012. www.dailymail.co.uk/news/article-2239072/Vampire-Sava-Savanovic-loose-Serbian-local-council-issues-public-health-warning.html.

de Groot, J. J. M. *The Religious System of China*. Vol. 5. Leiden, The Netherlands: E. J. Brill, 1907. https://books.google.com/books?id=lr1ZAAAAMAAJ.

Dickens, David B, and Elizabeth Miller. "Michel Beheim, German *Meistergesang*, and Dracula." *Journal of Dracula Studies* 5 (2003). Posted at Journal of Dracula Studies Archives. Kutztown University English Department. https://kutztownenglish.files.wordpress.com/2015/09/jds_v5_2003_dickens_and_miller.pdf.

Dodd, Kevin. "'Blood Suckers Most Cruel': The Vampire and the Bat in and before Dracula." Accessed on Academia.edu November 20, 2017. www.academia.edu/27682302/_Blood_Suckers_Most_Cruel_The_Vampire_and_the_Bat_in_and_before_Dracula.

Elworthy, Frederick Thomas. *The Evil Eye: An Account of This Ancient & Widespread Superstition*. London: John Murray, 1895. https://books.google.com/books?id=yIdAAAAYAAJ.

Encyclopædia Britannica, s.v. "Vampire Bat." Article published March 10, 2014. www.britannica.com/animal/vampire-bat.

Evans, E. P. "Superstition and Crime." In *Appletons' Popular Science Monthly* Vol. 54. Edited by William Jay Youmans, 206–21. New York: D. Appleton, 1899. https://books.google.com/books?id=tJVJAAAAYAAJ.

"Existing Superstitions." *Andrew County Republican* (Savannah, MO), March 12, 1875. Accessed on Chronicling America: Historic American Newspapers, Library of Congress. http://chroniclingamerica.loc.gov/lccn/sn85034076/1875-03-12/ed-1/seq-6/.

Ferguson, Jonathan. "History at Stake! The Story behind Vampire Slaying Kits." *British Library English and Drama Blog*, November 14, 2014. http://blogs.bl.uk/english-and-drama/2014/11/history-at-stake-vampire-slaying-at-the-british-library.html.

France. "The Vampire of Snowdon." In *Bye-gones: Relating to Wales and the Border Counties, 1889–90*. 2nd ser., vol. 1. Edited by John Askew Roberts, 307. Oswestry, UK: Woodall, Minshall, 1890. https://books.google.com/books?id=ht4GAAAAYAAJ.

Frazer, J. G. *The Golden Bough: A Study in Magic and Religion*. Vol. 9. 3rd ed. London: Macmillan, 1913. https://books.google.com/books?id=lNM3AQAAMAAJ.

Frazer, J. G. *The Golden Bough: A Study in Magic and Religion*. Vol. 3. 3rd ed. London: Macmillan, 1914. https://books.google.com/books?id=f9w3AQAAMAAJ.

Gerard, Emily. *The Land beyond the Forest*. Vol. 1, *Facts, Figures, and Fancies from Transylvania*. Edinburgh: William Blackwood and Sons, 1888. https://books.google.com/books?id=nDY_AAAAYAAJ.

Gerard, Emily. "Transylvanian Superstitions." *Nineteenth Century* 18 (1885): 130–50. Reprinted in Emily Gerard and Agnes Murgoci, *Transylvanian Superstitions*. Scripta Minora, 2013.

"Grabesschändung hilft gegen Cholera." *Neues Wiener Abendblatt* (Vienna, Austria) 213 (August 4, 1873). In *Neues Wiener Tagblatt 1873*. https://books.google.com/books?id=5ZM396nN_gIC.

Guiley, Rosemary Ellen. *The Encyclopedia of Vampires & Werewolves*. 2nd ed. New York: Checkmark Books, 2011.

Harley, Timothy. *Moon Lore*. London: Swan Sonnenschein, Le Bas, & Lowrey, 1885. https://books.google.com/books?id=ShwHAAAAQAAJ.

"Hawthorn." In *Chamber's Encyclopædia: A Dictionary of Universal Knowledge*. Vol. 5. London: William and Robert Chambers, 1897. https://books.google.com/books?id=QYJRAAAAYAAJ.

Haxthausen, Baron von. *Transcaucasia: Sketches of the Nations and Races between the Black Sea and the Caspian*. London: Chapman & Hall, 1854. https://books.google.com/books?id=Qvs9AAAAcAAJ.

Haydn, Joseph. *Dictionary of Dates, and Universal Reference*. 2nd ed. London: Edward Moxon, 1844. https://books.google.com/books?id=riU-AAAAYAAJ.

Johnson, Nicholas, Nidia Aréchiga-Ceballos, and Alvaro Aguilar-Setien. "Vampire Bat Rabies: Ecology, Epidemiology and Control." *Viruses* 6, no. 5 (May 2014): 1911–28. www.ncbi.nlm.nih.gov/pmc/articles/PMC4036541/.

Jovanovic, Dragana. "Vampire Threat Terrorizes Serbian Village." *ABC News*, November 29, 2012. http://abcnews.go.com/International/vampire-threat-terrorizes-serbian-village/story?id=17831327.

Kelly, Walter K. *Curiosities of Indo-European Tradition and Folk-Lore*. London: Chapman & Hall, 1863. https://books.google.com/books?id=2XXYAAAAMAAJ.

Kingston, William H. G., S. E. De Morgan, Martin Doyle, et al. "The Vampire; or, Pedro Pacheco and the Bruxa." In *Tales for All Ages*. By William H. G. Kingston, S. E. De Morgan, Martin Doyle, et al., 72–80. London: Bickers & Bush, 1863. https://books.google.com/books?id=XwgGAAAAQAAJ.

Klinger, Leslie S. "The Context of Dracula." In *The New Annotated Dracula*. By Bram Stoker. Edited by Leslie S. Klinger, xix–xix. New York: W. W. Norton, 2008.

Knoop, Otto. "Sagen aus Kujawien." *Zeitschrift des Vereins für Volkskunde* 16 (1906): 96–100. https://books.google.com/books?id=C2QKAAAAIAAJ.

Leake, William Martin. *Travels in Northern Greece*. Vol. 4. London: J. Rodwell, 1835. https://books.google.com/books?id=k0AVtzlZky0C.

Leland, Charles Godfrey. *Etruscan Roman Remains in Popular Tradition*. London: T. Fisher Unwin, 1892. https://books.google.com/books?id=zaFJAAAAMAAJ.

MacCulloch, J. A. "Vampire." In *Encyclopædia of Religion and Ethics*. Vol. 12, *Suffering–Zwingli*. Edited by James Hastings, 589–91. New York: Charles Scribner's Sons, 1922. https://books.google.com/books?id=UD8TAAAAYAAJ.

McNally, Raymond T. *Dracula: Truth and Terror*. Irvington, NY: Voyager, 1996. CD-ROM.

Melton, J. Gordon. *The Vampire Book: The Encyclopedia of the Undead*. 3rd ed. Detroit: Visible Ink, 2011.

Miller, Elizabeth. "Filing for Divorce: Count Dracula vs Vlad Tepes." In *Dracula: The Shade and the Shadow*. Edited by Elizabeth Miller. Westcliff-on-Sea, UK: Desert Island Books, 1998. Posted at Dracula's Homepage, 2005, www.ucs.mun.ca/~emiller/divorce.html.

More, Henry. *An Antidote against Atheism, or An Appeal to the Naturall Faculties of the Mind of Man, Whether There Be Not a God*. London: J. Flesher, 1655. https://books.google.com/books?id=gTdOAAAAcAAJ.

Murgoci, Agnes. "The Vampire in Roumania." *Folklore* 37, no. 4 (1926): 320–349, Reprinted in Emily Gerard and Agnes Murgoci, *Transylvanian Superstitions*. Scripta Minora, 2013.

"The Mysterious Stranger." In *Chambers's Repository of Instructive and Amusing Tracts*. Vol. 8. Edinburgh: W. and R. Chambers, 1854. https://books.google.com/books?id=MQ0bAAAAYAAJ.

Newburgh, Willelmi Parvi de. *Historia Rerum Anglicarum*. Vol. 2. London: Sumptibus Societatis, 1856. https://books.google.com/books?id=tOY9AAAAcAAJ.

Newburgh, William of. *The History of William of Newburgh: The Chronicles of Robert de Monte*. In *The Church Historians of England*. Vol. 4, part 2. Translated by Joseph Stevenson. London: Seeleys, 1856. https://books.google.com/books?id=dBQ5AQAAMAAJ.

Otelo. "Vampire Killing Essentials." *Ripley's Believe It or Not!* March 13, 2015. www.ripleys.com/weird-news/vampire-killing-kit/.

Otelo. "Vampire Killing Kits with Charles & Allie." *Ripley's Believe It or Not!* September 30, 2015. www.ripleys.com/weird-news/vampire-killing-kits.

Ovid. *The Metamorphoses of Ovid.* Vol. 1. Translated by Henry T. Riley. Philadelphia: David McKay, 1899. https://books.google.com/books?id=W4YXAAAAIAAJ.

Patrick, Nickolette. "Bacteria with Fangs." *Northeastern Spotlight* 4, no. 3 (Fall 2009): 6–7. http://globaltb.njms.rutgers.edu/downloads/products/RTMCCSpotlight-Fall2009.pdf.

Perkowski, Jan Louis. *Vampire Lore: From the Writings of Jan Louis Perkowski.* Bloomington, IN: Slavica, 2006.

Petrescu, Monica. "The Long Shadow of Dracula." *The Telegraph*, February, 6, 2005. www.telegraph.co.uk/news/worldnews/europe/romania/1482941/The-long-shadow-of-Dracula.html.

Philostratus. *The Life of Appolonius of Tyana: The Epistles of Apollonius and the Treatise of Eusebius.* Vol. 1. Translated by F. C. Conybeare. London: William Heinemann, 1912. https://books.google.com/books?id=nzghyc2nJbMC.

Pliny (the Elder). *The Natural History of Pliny.* Vol. 4. Translated by John Bostock and H. T. Riley. London: Henry G. Bohn, 1856. https://books.google.com/books?id=IUoMAAAAIAAJ.

Polidori, John William. *The Vampyre: A Tale.* London: Sherwood, 1819. https://books.google.com/books?id=ZMsBAAAAQAAJ.

Pouqueville, F. C. *Travels in the Morea, Albania, and Other Parts of the Ottoman Empire.* Translated by Anne Plumptre. London: Henry Colburn, 1813. https://books.google.com/books?id=Ar9BAAAAYAAJ.

Ralston, W. R. S. *Russian Folk-Tales.* New York: R. Worthington, 1880. https://books.google.com/books?id=LTMYAAAAYAAJ.

Ralston, W. R. S. *The Songs of the Russian People: As Illustrative of Slavonic Mythology and Russian Social Life.* London: Ellis & Green, 1872. https://books.google.com/books?id=6EFLAAAAYAAJ.

Resneck, Jacob. "Serbs Hope Vampire Lore Will Scare Up Some More Tourists." *USA TODAY*, December 28, 2012. www.usatoday.com/story/news/world/2012/12/27/vampire-scare/1770213/.

"The Restless Dead: Vampires and Decomposition." *Bizarre Magazine*, May–June 1997. Posted at Dr. Mark Benecke, International Forensic Research & Consulting. August 21, 2015. http://home.benecke.com/publications/the-restless-dead-vampires-and-decomposition.

Rodd, Rennell. *The Customers and Lore of Modern Greece.* 2nd ed. London: David Stott, 1892. https://books.google.com/books?id=k-fYAAAAMAAJ.

Rymer, James Malcolm, or Thomas Preskett Prest. *Varney the Vampire; or, The Feast of Blood.* London: E. Lloyd, 1847. www.gutenberg.org/ebooks/14833.

Skal, David J. *V Is for Vampire: The A–Z Guide to Everything Undead.* New York: Penguin Group, 1996.

Skeat, Walter William. *Malay Magic: Being an Introduction to the Folklore and Popular Religion of the Malay Peninsula.* London: MacMillan, 1900. https://books.google.com/books?id=AOc-AAAAYAAJ.

St. Clair, S. G. B., and Charles A. Brophy. *A Residence in Bulgaria.* London: John Murray, 1869. https://books.google.com/books?id=U5FMAAAAcAAJ.

Stojanovic, Dusan. "Vampire on the Loose in Serbia?" *Daily Local News*, December 1, 2012. www.dailylocal.com/article/DL/20121201/NEWS05/121209975.

Stoker, Bram. *Bram Stoker's Notes for Dracula: A Facsimile Edition.* Edited by Robert Eighteen-Bisang and Elizabeth Miller. Jefferson, NC: McFarland, 2008.

Stoker, Bram. *Dracula.* 6th ed. Westminster, UK: Archibald Constable, 1899. https://books.google.com/books?id=hhBEAQAAMAAJ.

Stott, Andre McConnell. "The Poet, the Physician and the Birth of the Modern Vampire." *Public Domain Review.* Accessed August 1, 2016. https://publicdomainreview.org/2014/10/16/the-poet-the-physician-and-the-birth-of-the-modern-vampire.

Summers, Montague. *The Vampire in Europe.* New Hyde Park, NY: University Books, 1961. Reprinted as *The Vampire in Lore and Legend* (Mineola, NY: Dover, 2013).

Summers, Montague. *The Vampire, His Kith and Kin.* New York: E. P. Dutton, 1929. Reprinted as *Vampires and Vampirism* (Mineola, NY: Dover, 2005)

Tournefort, Joseph Pitton de. *A Voyage into the Levant*. Vol. 1. London: D. Midwinter, 1741. https://books.google.com/books?id=Bgk-AQAAMAAJ.

Tozer, Henry Fanshawe. *Researches in the Highlands of Turkey: Including Visits to Mount Ida, Athos, Olympus, and Pelion, to the Mirdite Albanians, and Other Remote Tribes*. Vol. 2. London: John Murray, 1869. https://books.google.com/books?id=vFxCAAAAcAAJ.

"The Travels of Three English Gentlemen, from Venice to Hamburgh, Being the Grand Tour of Germany, in the Year 1734." In *The Harleian Miscellany; or, A Collection of Scarce, Curious, and Entertaining Pamphlets and Tracts, as Well in Manuscript as in Print, Found in the Late Earl of Oxford's Library, Interspersed with Historical, Political, and Critical Notes*. Vol. 4. Edited by William Oldys, 348–59. London: T. Osborne, 1745. https://books.google.com/books?id=X11UAAAAcAAJ.

"Vampire." In *Chamber's Encyclopædia: A Dictionary of Universal Knowledge for the People*. Vol. 9. American rev. ed. Edited by Ephraim Chambers, Robert Chambers, and William Chambers, 708–709. Philadelphia: J. B. Lippincott, 1883. https://books.google.com/books?id=vZ0MAAAAYAAJ.

"Vampire." In *The New International Encyclopædia*. Vol. 23, *Valjean–Zyrians*. 2nd ed. Edited by Daniel C. Gilman, Harry T. Peck, and Frank M. Colby, 8–9. New York: Dodd, Mead, 1917. https://books.google.com/books?id=kIxIAQAAMAAJ.

"The Vampyre: A Tale by Lord Byron." *New Monthly Magazine* 1, no. 63 (April 1, 1819). Reprinted in *The New Monthly Magazine and Universal Register*. Vol. 11 (London: Henry Colburn, 1819). https://books.google.com/books?id=VCQ8AQAAMAAJ.

Vukanović, T. P. "The Vampire." In *Vampire Lore: From the Writings of Jan Louis Perkowski*. 230–59. Bloomington, IN: Slavica, 2006.

"Witchcraft." In *Encyclopædia of Superstitions, Folklore, and the Occult Sciences of the World*. Vol. 3. Edited by Cora Linn Daniels and C. M. Stevens, 1445–69. Milwaukee, WI: J. H. Yewdale & Sons, 1903. https://books.google.com/books?id=ns0gK0efOvYC.

Wright, Dudley. *Vampires and Vampirism*. 2nd ed. London: W. Rider & Son, 1924. Reprinted as *The Book of Vampires* (Mineola, NY: Dover, 2006).

Zaslaw, Diana, dir. *Vampire Secrets*. DVD. New York: A&E Television Networks, 2006.

Index

A. P. SYLVIA

has long had an interest in supernatural
beliefs and their origins. Beyond just
immersing himself in the essential texts of
vampire folklore, he has traveled to a
number of vampire-related locations. He is
a member of the Transylvanian Society of
Dracula (North American chapter) as well
as The Dracula Society (based in London).
He runs the website LocationsOfLore.com
and is a fan of classic monster movies.